The Gathas
of Zarathushtra

The Gathas of Zarathushtra

Hymns in Praise of Wisdom

Translation and Commentary by Piloo Nanavutty

Mapin Publishing, Ahmedabad

First published in India
in 1999 by
Mapin Publishing Pvt. Ltd.
Chidambaram, Ahmedabad 380013 India
web-site: www.mapinpub.com

Simultaneously published in the
United States of America in 1999 by
Grantha Corporation
80 Cliffedgeway, Middletown, NJ 07701

Distributed in North America by
Antique Collectors' Club
Market Street Industrial Park
Wappingers' Falls, NY 12590
Tel: 800-252-5321 • Fax: 914-297-0068
web-site: www.antiquecc.com

Distributed in the United Kingdom & Europe by
Antique Collectors' Club
5 Church Street, Woodbridge
Suffolk IP12 1DS
Tel: 1394-385-501 • Fax: 1394-384-434
email: accvs@aol.com

ISBN: 1-890206-09-1 pb (Grantha)
ISBN: 1-890206-11-3 hb (Grantha)
ISBN: 81-85822-56-5 pb (Mapin)
ISBN: 81-85822-58-1 hb (Mapin)
LC: 98-68330

Edited by Shernaz Cama
Designed by Paulomi Shah/
Mapin Design Studio
Printed in India by Ajanta Offset, New Delhi

Jacket illustration:

The Emblem on the Cover represents a
Sasanian Fire Altar with its triple base
standing for the motto of the religion: Good
Thoughts, Good Words, Good Deeds. The
horse with forelegs raised represents the
spirit of ascending prayer.

Frontispiece:

Stained glass window depicting the Prophet.
Fire-Temple, Bandra, Bombay

Translator's Note

I have been fascinated by *The Gathas of Zarathushtra* from my student days. Even after the publication of *Songs of Zarathushtra,* co-authored by the late Dastur Dr. Framroze Ardeshir Bode (Allen & Unwin 1952), my research continued. This new edition would not exist but for the generous help given to me by Farrokh Jal Vajifidar of London. Together we have combed through the Gathas, word by word, line by line, stanza by stanza, till he was satisfied. Seven summers passed by and if, in spite of such scrutiny, there are still lapses, the fault is entirely mine.

Farrokh also collected the major Pahlavi references to Gaush Urva, the Soul of the Cow and placed this material, in English translation at my disposal. I was able, therefore, to summarise the Story of Creation, as presented in the Legend of Gaush Urva, and make it the opening chapter of my translation, followed by the Lament of Gaush Urva (Ys.29), which it illuminates. Next comes Yasna 28, Zarathushtra at Prayer, after which the traditional order of the verses is maintained.

Further insights I owe to Farrokh have been acknowledged wherever they occur.

May the reader enjoy this most ancient of texts, as relevant today as when it was first composed centuries ago. *Ushta té!* Happiness to you!

P.N.

Dedicated

to

the late Dastur Dr. Framroze Ardeshir Bode,

who inspired in me a lasting love of the Gathas

and

to

Farrokh Jal Vajifdar, friend, critic, Hamkar or

fellow-traveller on the Path of Truth

Contents

Acknowledgements

My grateful thanks go to the Sponsors of this book, Jamshed and Shirin Guzder, Dr. Sorab M. Jhaveri, Mr. Cyrus J. Guzder and Mr. Farokh J. Guzder as Trustees of Jerbai Cowasji Dinshaw Adenwalla Trust, the Delhi Parsi Anjuman, and to my Irani Zoroastrian friends who wish to remain anonymous; to the Bibliothèque Nationale, Paris; and the Metropolitan Museum of Art, New York, for permission to reproduce rare material in their possession; to the Librarians and staff of the K.R. Cama Oriental Institute, Bombay; the School of Oriental and African Studies, London; Indian Institute of Islamic Studies, Delhi; Nehru University Library, India International Centre and the Indira Gandhi National Centre for the Arts, Delhi, for their courtesy and ever-ready help.

I am indebted to Professor Emeritus Dr. Mary Boyce, and to Professor Emeritus Dr. Kaikhushrov D. Irani and his wife, Piroja, for much kindness and encouragement; to Dastur Dr. K.M. Jamaspasa, Head Priest of the Anjuman Atash Behram, Bombay, for helpful suggestions; to Dr. Miss Sabar Havewalla, Head of the Centre of Persian and Central Asian Studies, School of Languages, Nehru University, Delhi, for vigorous discussions and for consenting to translate this book into Farsi/Persian. To Dr. Chandra Rajan for her help with the Sanskrit references, and to Russi Billimoria for his suggestions adopted in the Introduction, my grateful thanks.

My warm thanks to the artists Vinubhai Trivedi, Nirmal Sarteja, Frenny Billimoria, Mehroo J. Wadia and Ketayun Saklath for their contributions. To Jehangir R. Patel, Editor, *Parsiana Journal,* to Roshan R. Rivetna, Editor, FEZANA Journal, to Mr. Jamshed Guzder, President of the Federation of Parsi Zoroastrian Anjumans of India, to Lt. Gen. A. M. Sethna, President, Delhi Parsi Anjuman, and to all members of my own Delhi Anjuman as also to Keki Gandhi, Editor, *Fed. Newsletter*, my gratitude for their cordiality and support.

To my Publishers, Mapin Publishing Pvt. Ltd. and their representatives, Bipin Shah and Paulomi Shah, and to my brilliant young Editor, Dr. Shernaz Cama, my sincere thanks for their patience and close cooperation at every step in preparing this publication; to my students for their interest and questioning without which this book would not be what it is, my warm thanks.

Last, but not least, to my own family I owe a great debt of gratitude: To my husband, Nowshir, whose Fravashi (Guardian Spirit), is ever by my side, consoling and encouraging me at every turn and to my dearest of sons, Hoshang, whose love, generosity and interest in his mother's work can never be repaid, to my sisters, Pareen Lalkaka and Dina Nanavutty, my niece, Aban, and grandniece, Anahita, to my husband's sisters, Dr. Amy C. Bhabha, Dr. Jean J. Moos, Scylla R. Vatcha and Tehmie N. Guzder, my warmest thanks for their loving support.

Foreword

I am delighted by the request of Piloo Nanavutty (Mrs. P. N. Jungalwalla) asking me to write the Foreword to her book, *The Gathas of Zarathushtra, Hymns in Praise of Wisdom*. I take this opportunity to pay my humble tribute to the great Zoroastrian tradition which has made the Indian rainbow resplendent for more than a thousand years.

The *Gathas* unfold Zarathushtra's vision with a vibrant and poetic resonance. Each hymn enshrines the distilled essence of his total dedication to Ahura Mazda, embodiment of Life and Wisdom. The Prophet of ancient Iran extols the divine attributes which form the core of his faith. These are: *Vohu Mana*, Good Mind, unique in the history of world religions; *Asha*, (Vedic *Rta*), Truth and Cosmic Order; *Kshathra* (Vedic *Kshatra*), Power, Sovereignty; *Armaiti*, (Vedic *Armaiti*), Devotion based on Rightmindedness, not thoughtless devotion; and the twins: *Haurvatat*, (Vedic *Sarvatat*), Perfection, and *Ameretat*, (Vedic *Amrutatat*), Immortality. In the *Gathas*, as in the Vedas, the Sun is the symbol of Truth and Wisdom. Fire is an emblem of the Divine, and is the sacred witness at all ceremonies, Zoroastrian and Vedic. The many-faceted symbol of Gaush Urva/Geush Urva, which may be translated as the Soul of the Cow or Bull or Earth is explained in depth in this study.

Zarathushtra describes himself as a *Manthran*, preacher of the *Manthra* (Vedic *Mantra*), the Sacred Word of Power. He claims to be an *ereshi*, (Vedic rishi), who foresees "what will or will not be" (*Yasna*, 31.5).

I am confident that this publication will be conducive to collaborative research by Avesta and Vedic Scholars in common pursuit of understanding and interpreting the ancient roots of our civilization.

The book is illustrated by images collected from varied sources. The Introduction, Commentaries, Translation with Glossary, Bibliography and Index will help the common reader to enjoy the *Gathas* and perceive their relevance to our daily life.

Dr. L. M. Singhvi, M. P.
Former High Commissioner of India to the U. K.

Introduction

The Gathas are devotional songs composed in intricate verse by Zarathushtra or Zoroaster as the Greeks named him, Prophet of ancient Iran. Zarathushtra is believed to be the first in human history to have founded a religion based on the ethical values of Truth and Justice named **Asha** (Vedic *Rta*) in the Gathas. He preached one Supreme God, **Ahura Mazda**, Lord of Life and Wisdom, to be worshipped in thought, word and deed for the protection and evolution of Man and Nature. His followers are called Zoroastrians in the West and Zartoshtis in the East. These last include the Parsis of India and the Zartoshtis of Iran.

Although the religion taught by Zarathushtra is considered the most ancient of the revealed religions, it is the least known. This is due to various reasons. Out of a vast literature divided into 21 Nasks or Divisions, seven books on Religion, seven on Statecraft and seven on Medicine, which once existed under the Sasanians (226-651 AC) only one fifth survives, and that too is incomplete, with many books missing. The invasion of Iran by Alexander the Great in 330 BC, resulted in the deliberate destruction of many religious texts, and the death of many learned priests. When Alexander died in 323 BC, forty years of turmoil followed. Eventually, after the Battle of Ipsus (301 BC), the Persian empire was divided into three monarchies: The Macedonian in Europe; the Ptolemaic in Egypt and the Seleucid in Asia.[1]

The Seleucids were followed by the Parthian Arsacids (160 BC-225 AC). The Greeks were evicted by the Parthian Arsacids in 150 BC after which there was a revival of the Zoroastrian religion. King Valkash, generally identified with the Arsacid King Vologese I (c.51-79 AC), ordered a search for all the surviving portions of the scattered *Avesta*, or the Sacred Scriptures of the Zoroastrians, and had these as well as all the prayers of the oral tradition recited by heart for centuries, written down. About this time, the Royal Seal affixed to official documents begins to have the Pahlavi Arsacid script on one side and a Zoroastrian Fire Altar on the other. A large number of these seals can be examined in the magnificent collection housed in the British Library, London.

The good work started by King Valkash was continued by the Kings of the Sasanian Dynasty, the final redaction of the *Avesta* being completed some time in the sixth century.

The second invasion of Iran by the Arabs was even more disastrous than that of Alexander. At the Battle of Nihavand (641 AC), the last Iranian King, Yazdegird III, fled to Merv where he hid for ten years before he was discovered and assassinated by one of his own generals. The collapse of the Sasanian Empire was complete. Not only were Fire Temples destroyed, religious texts burnt, Zoroastrian priests killed, but, in due course, Arabic replaced the Persian language. Those who still clung to their ancient faith hid in mountain caves and remote desert areas. Finally, about the middle of the tenth century, a few migrated to India and settled there forming the community of the Parsis, people from Pars or Fars in Southern Iran.

It is not known exactly when Zarathushtra lived or when the Gathas were composed. The Greeks considered him a very ancient prophet and placed him around 6000 BC, considered untenable. Yet some startling facts are revealed by a 115 member international team of scientists examining the mummified body of "the iceman of Tyrol" discovered by German tourists on the 19th of September, 1991. The iceman and his belongings are dated c. 5,300 BC, late Neolithic or Copper Age. A "sophisticated" Copper axe was found beside the frozen figure. Till recently it was held that copper and zinc were mined c.3,500 BC, iron ore c.1000 BC, yet these discoveries pre-date the mining of copper by two thousand years. The veteran archaeologist, Paul G. Bahn, in his recent study on Prehistoric Art, asserts that iron oxide was discovered in South Africa and Australia C. 45,000-50,000 B.C in Hungary C. 30,000 B.C and much later in France and Portugal.

In the Gathas, the ordeal by molten metal is mentioned in Ys.32.7; 51.9, while a deadly "weapon" is referred to in Ys.31.18. There is, therefore, a strong probability that the molten metal

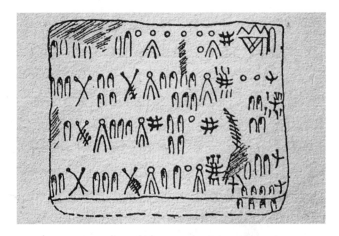

Fig.1

**Proto-Elamite
Script** c. 3000 BC

Fig.1A

**Semi Picto-graphic
Script**
Mohenjodaro
Museum
Lead Paper weight
(Private Collection)

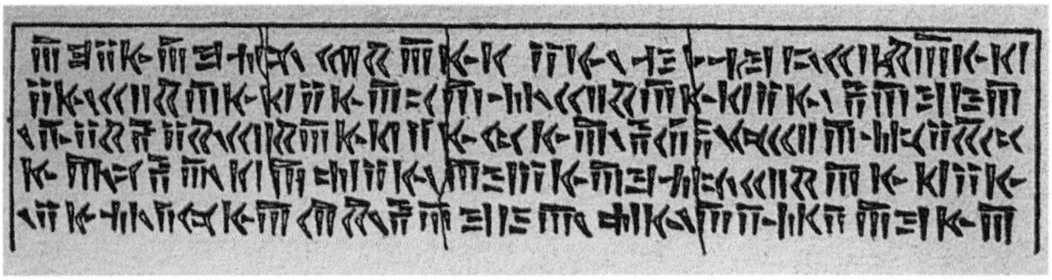

Fig.2

Cuneiform Script
Gold Tablet of
Ariaramnes
c. 640-590 BC

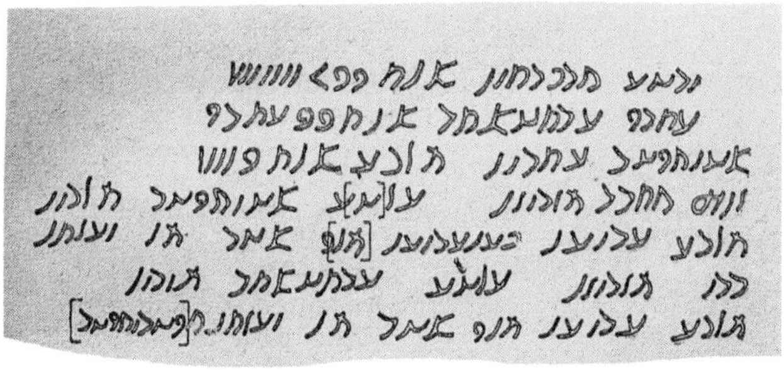

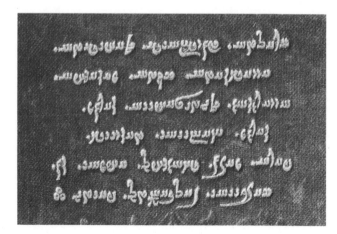

Fig.3

**Pahlavi Arsacid
Script** c. 400 BC

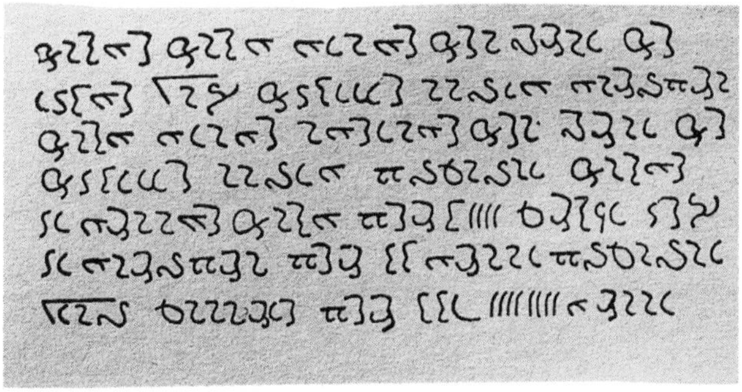

Fig.4

**Pahlavi Sasanian
Script**
c. 6th century AC

Fig.5

**Avesta Script of the
Gathas.**
Composed in
Sasanian Era
Lettering in Gold on
Cover of Gujarati
edition of *The
Gathas*, 1919.

mentioned by Zarathushtra points to copper, and not iron and the deadly "weapon" to a hatchet or "shafted" axe.[2]

Western scholars place Zarathushtra between 2000-1000 BC or later. Sasanian priests, under pressure of other religious groups, concocted a specific date, "258 years before Alexander conquered Iran" (330 BC). This works out to c. 600 BC.

Be that as it may, it is now acknowledged that Zoroastrian religious beliefs such as rewards and punishment, Heaven and Hell, the Resurrection of the Dead, a Last Judgement, the coming of the **Saoshyant,** a world saviour who will conquer Evil for ever, and finally, a Renewal of Existence when Man, Nature and all creatures are restored to their pristine glory, were beliefs which influenced Buddhism, Judaism, Christianity and Islam.

The language in which the Gathas are composed is called Gathic or Old Avestan to distinguish it from the later Avestan Texts known as the Younger Avesta. The Gathas have close affinities with the *Rig-Veda*. As Farrokh Jal Vajifdar remarks:

> "Indeed, the Vedas and later, the Upanishads, have been instrumental in shedding precious light on the frequent linguistic and occasional philosophic problems posed by this most difficult ancient Iranian tongue." (Unpublished paper)

The discovery of Middle Iranian documents from Central Asia at the beginning of the twentieth century helped to clarify many obscure aspects of Gathic Avestan. It was only in the fourth century of our era that an attempt was made to devise a script for the Gathas which were recited by heart from generation to generation by devoted priests and their followers. Thus a 48-character script was created to embody the sounds and cadences of Zarathushtra's *manthras*, "words of prophetic intent", which are the Gathas. This fourth century script of the Gathas was further modified under the four hundred year rule of the Sasanian Dynasty.

Zarathushtra is believed to have lived and taught in a

remote, fertile valley in the North-East of Iran. His highly inflected chants had to be modified to accommodate the vowel sounds and phonemic forms prevalent in South-Western Iran, specially the province of Fars, the very heart of Sasanian culture. The written language of the Sasanians was Pahlavi, their spoken language Pazand. A thousand years separated the composition of the Gathas from their first written script. During this period, not only did language change, but religious, political and social ideas had altered. It is, therefore extremely difficult to translate Zarathushtra's very own ideas. No wonder then that even eminent Gatha scholars, such as J. Duchesne-Guillemin, Helmut Humbach, Stanley Insler and Jean Kellens and his collaborator, Eric Pirart, differ from one another.

Roman Ghirshman, in his absorbing study, *Iran* (Pelican Books, 1954) points out that the Elamites were the first to devise some form of writing, c. 3000 BC. This was a marked advance from the semi-pictographic script found at Mohenjodaro and Harappa. (Fig.1 and 1A)

The Elamite script was further developed by the Iranians into the cuneiform script. A gold tablet discovered at Hamadan bears the following inscription by King Ariaramnes (c. 640-590 BC), brother of Cyrus the Great (640-600 BC):

> "I, Ariaramnes, great King, King of Kings, King of the land of Parsa. This land of the Persians which I possess, provided with fine horses and good men, it is the great god, Ahuramazda who has given it to me. I am King of this land."

Ghirshman explains:

> "This tablet is the oldest Achaemenian object known and bears the earliest Old Persian text. It shows the great progress that had been made by the beginning of the seventh century B.C. by Persian tribes who had but recently passed from the semi-nomadic state into that of a semi-sedentary people."   (Ghirshman, p. 120)

When the Parthian Arsacids came to power after the Battle of Ipsus, they further developed the cuneiform script into the Pahlavi Arsacid script (Ghirshman, p. 257, Fig. 3). During the long reign of the Sasanians (226-651 AC), the Pahlavi Arsacid script gave way to the Pahlavi Sasanian script. (Ghirshman, Fig.4) Finally, the Sasanians devised the beautiful Avesta script. For centuries the Gathas had been chanted by priests and laymen. At last, this ancient text was embodied in writing. In 1919 Kavasji Eduljee Kanga reproduced the Avesta script in gold lettering on the front cover of his *Gatha-ba-Mayeni*, Gujarati edition: Bombay. (Fig. 5).

The standard social and regional divisions in Zarathushtra's day were: **Demana/Nmana**, the home or house; **Vis**, the town; **Shoithra/Zantu**, the province or state; and **Dakhyu**, the country.

Society in Zarathushtra's day was divided into four categories. The most important was the **Zaotar** (Vedic *Zot*), the officiating priest at a ritual. He was assisted by the **Karapans**, (mumbler priests), who indulged in corrupt practices and got drunk on large quantities of Haoma, Vedic *Soma*. The second social group were named **Ratheshtar**, (lit. charioteer, from Skt. *rath* chariot) the warrior, skilled in the use of mace, javelin, spear, sling. They were represented by the **Kavis**, the Princelings. They too were often corrupt and under the influence of the Karapans, with the noble exception of Kavi **Vishtaspa**, Zarathushtra's patron. The third category were the **Fashuyente** and **Vastriya**, herdsman and husbandman. They were the backbone of the community and their wealth consisted of herds of cattle as also a few sheep and goats. Camels and horses were bred for chariot racing and for transport. In the fourth category came the **Huiti**, craftsmen. They were chiefly blacksmiths and leather workers.

Zarathusthra describes himself as a Zaotar, (Ys.33.6). He identifies himself with the oppressed herdsman, and with the **Drighu**, the poor and the downtrodden (Ys.34.5, 53.9). His followers too are divided into the following groups. The most advanced were the **Khvaetu**, the self-reliant, or strong in spirit. Among them were the **Vidvao**, the learned ones (Cf. Skt. *vidhvan purusha*, the learned man). Next came the **Verezena**, the community of the faithful from all walks of life. Lastly, there were the **Airyamna**, the Arya Clan. Bartholomae keeps to three broad divisions: the Family, the Community and the Clan.

A great deal of pastoral imagery is found in the Gathas. *Gava azi*, cows-in-calf, signifies plenty and prosperity. Proper names include "aspa", horse, and "ushtra"/"ostra", camel, as, for example, Jamaspa, Frashaoshtra. Zarathushtra spoke at different metaphoric levels depending upon his audience. To the herdsman he uses such phrases like "the joy-giving cow" (Humbach), "cattle, the source of good fortune" (Duchesne-Guillemin). To the Kavis, some of whom were learned in composing mantric verses and familiar with their folklore and history, he would use imagery such as "the sun of wisdom and Truth".

Let us now turn to the life of Zarathushtra as depicted in the Pahlavi Texts.

Zarathushtra:

There is no authentic life of Zarathushtra, but traditional accounts exist. These are found in the Pahlavi Texts, such as *Dinkart* (Acts of the Religion), *Selections from Zadspram*, a learned and much travelled priest of the Sasanian Era, the *Zarthusht-nama* and other texts carefully analysed by the Yugoslav scholar, Marijan Mole.[3]

According to the Pahlavi texts, Zarathushtra's family name was Spitama, after his ninth ancestor. The word Spitama means very white. The title, Zarathushtra, was probably given to him when he became known for his teaching. His father was Pourushaspa, owner of many horses, and his mother was Dughdova, milkmaid (cf. Skt. *dughda*, milk). Dughdova's father was a saintly man named Frahim-rava. When his daughter was fifteen years old, a beautiful, golden light surrounded her day and night. The villagers thought she was bewitched and wanted to kill her. Frahim-rava, therefore, sent her away to his friend, Paitiraspa, lord of horses who lived in Arak. Paitiraspa married her to his son, Pourushaspa.

Miracles abound in the Prophet's life. When he was born, it is said that he laughed whereas other children cry. In the *Farvardin Yasht* (Yt.13.93-94), we are told that the whole of Nature rejoiced at the birth of the Prophet. Pliny (23-79 AC), in his *Natural History*, writes that the vibrations of the child's head were so strong that no hand could be laid on it. A black magician, Dorasarun, and his followers made several attempts to kill the child. He was kidnapped and thrown among a herd of cattle to be trampled to death, but a sturdy cow stood over him till his mother found her babe and took him home. Again, he was thrown into a burning pit, but the flames cooled. His mother found him playing among the flames and took him home. Then Dorasarun and his men placed the child in a wolf's lair after the baby wolves had been slain. When the wolf pair returned, they wanted to devour the infant, but their jaws locked and they were paralysed. A pair of she-goats passed by and carried the babe with them. At last, Dughdova found him and took her son home. One last attempt was made by Dorasarun himself. He crept into the bedchamber of the sleeping child, javelin in hand, but as he lifted the weapon his hand was paralysed. The javelin fell to the floor with a clatter. He fled.

At the age of twenty Zarathushtra is said to have left his home to meditate in a cave. His first vision of Ahura Mazda, Lord of Life and Wisdom, was received when he was thirty. Seven other visions, six communications with Ahura Mazda's Powers, later known as the **Amesha Spenta**, Immortal Shining Ones, or Benevolent Immortals, and a homiletic dialogue followed the first vision over a period of years.

His first convert was his own cousin, Maidhyomaongha, mentioned in the Gathas. The two men wandered from village to village, but none would listen to their preaching.

At long last they were invited by Kavi Vishtaspa, the ruling prince of Bactria (Afghanistan), to explain the new doctrine to him and his Court. For three days Zarathushtra preached his doctrine. But certain courtiers became jealous. They smuggled dead matter, human hair, bones, putrid nails, under the pillow of the Prophet who stayed at an inn. The terrified innkeeper was made to swear silence or else he would be killed. In open court, the noblemen accused the Prophet of being a black magician. The evidence was produced, Vishtaspa was enraged and ordered Zarathushtra to be flung into a dungeon. At that moment, the favourite horse of Vishtaspa, Aspa Siha, was rolling on the ground in agony as his four legs disappeared into his stomach. Not all the *hakims* of the land could cure him.

Zarathushtra heard this story from the Keeper of the Dungeon and offered to cure Aspa Siha. Permission was granted. After bathing, putting on clean clothes and saying his prayers, Zarathushtra presented himself at Court. Aspa Siha was carried into the court room. Before he would cure the horse, Zarathushtra laid down four conditions. The first was that Vishtaspa should embrace the new doctrine. Vishtaspa agreed. Then the Prophet stroked the right leg of Aspa Siha reciting certain prayers. Immediately the leg straightened and shot out. The second condition was that Zarathushtra be taken to the chambers of Queen Hutoxshi to whom he would explain the new faith, and if she was convinced of its truth, she should embrace it. Permission was granted. Zarathushtra convinced the Queen who gladly accepted the new faith. Zarathustra returned to the Court where he stroked the left leg of Aspa Siha, reciting certain prayers. That leg too straightened and shot out. The Prophet's third condition was that the Crown Prince, Asfandiar, be asked to swear on his sword that he would accept the new faith and spread it throughout the land and beyond. The Prince agreed. The third leg shot out as Zarathustra stroked it and recited certain prayers.

His last request was that the innkeeper be summoned and made to swear, on pain of death, to tell the truth as to how the putrid matter came to be under the pillow of the Prophet. The innkeeper was summoned and confessed the truth, pointing out those courtiers responsible for the act. Vishtaspa ordered the guilty courtiers to be beheaded, but Zarathushtra pleaded that they should be banished instead as that would be punishment enough. And so they were led out from the gates of the city to fend for themselves. Aspa Siha was completely cured.

Zarathushtra is said to have married Havovi, the daughter of Frashaoshtra, a senior courtier at Vishtaspa's court, and had by her three sons and three daughters. The marriage of his youngest daughter, Pouruchista, is celebrated in the last Gatha. Zarathushtra is described as being active in propagating the faith. He died a violent death at the age of seventy-seven years while at prayer in the Fire Temple at Balkh (Kabul) being killed by a hostile border chief, Tur-bara-Tur.

Turning back to the Gathas, we learn from the Greek historian, Pliny, who relied on the authority of Hermippus (c. 200 BC), that Zarathushtra composed "one million lines of verse."[4] Only a fragment of seventeen hymns, divided into five Gathas, survives.

The Gathas form part of the *Yasna*, a liturgical text of seventy-two chapters or **Haiti**. The Gathic sections are as follows:

Gatha Ahunavaiti	Ys.28–34 The Gatha of Free Choice
Gatha Ushtavaiti	Ys.43–46 The Gatha of Bliss, and Enlightenment;
Gatha Spenta Mainyu	Ys.47–50 The Gatha of the Holy Spirit ;
Gatha Vohu Khashathra	Ys.51 The Gatha of Sovereignty or the Good Kingdom
Gatha Vahishtoishti	Ys.53, The Gatha of the Highest Wish or Fulfilment.

Between the First and the Second Gatha is placed the *Yasna Haptanhaiti*, the Yasna of Seven Chapters Ys.35–41, in the Gathic dialect and in poetic prose, composed by the Gatha Community, early followers of the Prophet, after his death.

Yasna 42 is a brief supplement, a fragment of much later date and has no connection with the Gathas or the *Yasna Haptanhaiti*, (*Haptan Yasht*). Between the Fourth and the Fifth Gathas comes *Yasna* 52, a brief chapter describing the physical, mental and spiritual elements which make up the personality of every individual. (See *Body* in Glossary)

Zarashushtra was familiar with the *Vedas*. He knew how to compose mantric verses filled with meaning. He seems to be aware of the *Asuras*, high gods of Truth and Justice, before they were demonised in the later Hindu texts. He may have pondered over the Vedic word, *Médha*, wisdom. *Ahu* in Avestan signifies the indestructible life essence of Ahura, the Living One, and Ahura Mazda the Living Lord of Life and Wisdom. He has neither beginning nor end. He IS. He lives in **Anagra Raochao,** Everlasting Light.

He chose to create:

> Ahura Mazda's First Thought
> blazed into myriads of sparks of light
> and filled the entire heavens.
> He Himself, in His Wisdom,
> is the Creator of Truth which
> upholds His Supreme Mind.   (Ys.31.7)

> When I held You in my mind's eye,
> then I realised You, O Mazda,
> as the First and the Last for all Eternity,
> as the Father of Good Mind,
> the true Creator of Truth,
> and Lord over the actions of life.   (Ys.31.8)

Thus was born **getig**, the physical world, and **menog**, the mental world. To this day we live in this combined world of matter and spirit. Both are sacred.

Moreover, Ahura Mazda guides Man, Nature and the Cosmos through His six Powers which emanate from Him. These are:

Asha	Vedic *Rta*. Cosmic Order, Truth, Justice.
Vohu Mana	The Good Mind. No equivalent in any of the revealed religions or the Vedas.
Khashathra	Vedic *Kshatra*. Sovereignty, Power, Kingdom.
Armaiti	Vedic *Aramati*. Devotion, Love, Piety, Zeal.

Twins:
Haurvatat   Vedic *Sarvatat*. Health, Wellbeing, Perfection.
Ameretat   Vedic *Amrutatat*. Immortality.

The Twins have been compared to the Vedic *Asvins* or *Nasatyas*, the twin horsemen who ride beautiful, white horses their manes flying against blue skies. These handsome youths hold in their hands "madhu-vidya," the honey-sweet knowledge of Divinity, whch they bring down to earth. This gift makes "old men young again, and blind men see."

No wonder Zarathushtra makes the Gathic Twins, Perfection and Immortality, "dwell in the dazzling light" of Ahura Mazda's Wisdom (Ys.33.9), for it is through the "honey-sweet knowledge of Divinity" that Perfection and Immortality can be attained.

Closely associated with **Haurvatat** and **Ameretat** are Tevishi and Utayuiti respectively.

Tevishi, or Tavashi in the Vedas, is basically naked power. Hence, Zarathushtra uses the word in Ys. 29.1 as the brutality shown towards cattle by the society of his day.

In Ys. 33.12, however, Tevishi is given a totally different meaning. Here the word signifies moral courage or ardent desire for spiritual attainment. In post-Vedic texts, Tavishi is associated with *Kama Manas*, the Desire Mind. This longing can seek fulfilment by striving towards the Divine, or, it can degenerate into beastiality.

We can now understand why Zarathushtra uses the identical word, Tevishi, to signify at one time brutality, and at another the longing for Perfection.

I quote:

> Arise Within me, O Ahura,
> and fulfil my ardent desire (for Perfection)
> through unflinching Devotion.   (Ys.33.12)

Apparently, both meanings of the word were familiar to Zarathushtra's listeners.

Utayuiti is usually translated by scholars as endurance, perseverance or strength, depending on the context. I could not find an equivalent of utayuiti in the Vedas except for *uta* which is just a grammatical particle.

In the Gathas, all the above Powers interact with each other, the two most frequently mentioned being Asha and Vohu Mana. Later texts describe these as **Amesha Spenta** or **Haft Amshaspands**, Seven Benevolent Immortals, Ahura Mazda being the seventh who includes all.

Pervading each one of these are **Spenta Mainyu**, Ahura Mazda's ever-expanding Spirit of Benediction, and **Vahishta Mana**, His Supreme Mind.

According to Zoroastrian tradition, Plants, Animals and Man lived in perfect harmony with one another till **Angra Mainyu**, the Hostile Spirit, erupted from the bowels of the earth and poisoned existence.

Gaush Urva:

In the section entitled "The Legend of Gaush Urva" I have dramatised the story of the Creation and placed it before *Yasna* 29. Here I will summarise the various aspects of this multifarious symbol.

As the Sanskrit root, "go" or "gau" can be either masculine or feminine, some translators of the Gathas describe her as the Soul of the Cow, others as Ox-Soul or Soul of the Bull. Others again translate the phrase as Soul of the Kine or Cattle.

It is crucial to understand the oriental attitude to the Cow in contrast to the western attitude, for a full appreciation of this symbol.

In India, the Cow is a sacred animal and to this day is looked upon with great affection. A gentle, shy young girl is given the pet name, Gaurie, little cow. She is addressed in these words:

Aav mari garib Gai (Gujarati)
Aau méri garib Gau (Hindi)

Literally "Come here my gentle cow." The exact equivalent in English would be: "Come here my little lamb, my lambkin."

Turning back to the Gathas we find Gaush Urva complaining to Ahura Mazda in these words:

"For whom have You brought me into being?
Who shaped me?
Wrath and Rapine, Aggresion and Violence crush me
No one is my protector
except You, O Lord,
so reveal to me the caring herdsman."   (Ys.29.1)

In answer to her prayer, Zarathushtra is appointed as her protector and "blest with sweetness of speech" (Ys. 29.8). Gaush Urva, is not satisfied and wails that she must now submit "to the words of a feeble man" when she longed for a powerful warrior to help her with the "might of his hands" (Ys.29.9). But in the very next verse she blesses the Prophet and his followers and prays they may establish a peaceful existence through the Good Mind both for the herdsman and his herds and mankind (Ys.29.10).

This legend is also found in the tenth century Hindu text, the *Bhagvata Purana*, which is a commentary on the Gita. Mother Earth, "wearing the shape of Cow" goes before Indra, chief of the gods, and in the very words of Gaush Urva complains that she is oppressed and begs for a saviour. In answer to her prayer, the Lord Krishna is born (*Bhagvata Purana*, XI.17-18). The similarity is striking.

But the matter does not end here. In the Vedas, the cow is associated with the light of dawn, "Cows of dawn" being a Vedic image to which Harvey P. Alper, in his study *Mantra,* draws attention. He further quotes the phrase "the great face of the great (Gods) which leading the cows of dawn shall follow" (*RV.*I. 67, 5-6-9).[5]

Stanley Insler interprets Gaush Urva as the "Good Vision" though relegating this interpretation to footnotes.[6]

The phrase, *Ukshano asnam*, occurs twice in the Gathas, Ys.46.3; and 50.10, signifying the "glittering dawning of the days" which will herald the coming of the Saoshyants, the Saviours, who will uphold the "Truth-inspired existence" (Ys.46.3). Humbach translates *Ukshano asnam* as the "bulls of the days" keeping close to the Vedic imagery.[7]

There is a third aspect of Gaush Urva which is crucial to our understanding of the opening verse of the Gathas (Ys. 28.1). In the legend, she is the Soul of the Primeval Bull tortured to death by Angra Mainyu, the Hostile Spirit. She rises from his dead remains. In a voice like that *"of a thousand men calling out at one time"* she demands justice. Her anguished cry rings from one end of the Universe to the other. At "one stride" she reaches first the Stars, then the Moon, and lastly the Sun, and demands justice. They are helpless. Only Zarathushtra, appointed as her protector, will fight to bring justice to her and her herds.

The implication is that Zarathushtra extends his help not only to the suffering cattle, but also to the Drighu, the poor and the downtrodden who cry out for justice. Throughout the centuries Gaush Urva was held in great love and reverence by devout Zoroastrians. In a tenth century Pahlavi Text, the *Shayast-ne-Shayast* (The Proper and the Improper), she is raised to the status of an Amesha Spenta or Amshaspand a title reserved only for Ahura Mazda's first six powers:

May Amshapand Goshurun (Gaush Urva) be the protector of all four-footed creatures. (XXII.14)

Zarathushtra identifies himself with the poor and the oppressed. Hence the need to invoke the Wisdom of the Good Mind so that he can inspire them to fight for their rights (Ys.28.1).

For this reason he is persecuted by the corrupt princelings (Kavis) and equally corrupt priests (Karapans). He is in despair:

"To what land shall I flee? Where can I turn for refuge?
They have excluded me from family and clan.
 Nor does the community seek to rejoice me,
nor by any chance the wicked despots of the land…" (Ys.46.1)

He confesses that the "evil-minded chieftain, Bendva," has oppressed him because he tried to get justice due to the poor and the persecuted. (Ys.49.1). He therefore implores Ahura Mazda for help.

He concludes the poetic chapter, "Questionings", with this revealing verse:

"How, O Mazda,
Could the Daeva-worshipper ever have been good rulers?
I ask this
on behalf of those whom the Karapans and the Usiksh
have oppressed,
delivering the herds to Wrath.
The Kavis too are cruel to Gaush Urva
causing her constant pain and misery.
Nor do they approach Truth
to cultivate pastures for her well-being."   (Ys.44.20)

Zarathushtra warns the people of the consequences of this continued brutality: "Mazda has foretold the evil they will suffer when they destroy the life of the Cow with exultant shrieks" (Ys.32.12).

He also condemns **Yima** (Vedic *Yama*), son of Vivanghvant (Vedic *Vivasvat*) as a notorious sinner (Ys.32.8). He allowed the Bull Sacrifice to gratify the desire of his people who believed they would attain immortality by eating the consecrated flesh of the slain Bull. The concluding sentence of the verse, however, is unambiguous: "I separate myself from such sinners knowing what will come to them at the Final Judgment, O Mazda."

19

उपवशातानांॽउपरथरेॽणांॽातातांॽभा
फ़ॽतेनरौॽलंॽउपवशातोॽपडीॽमनर्मांॽथात्या
ॽउव्वाशॽतेयेॽपाषीॽशाॽत्नॽथीॽशोॽधी
काॽउॽॽपाॽशातॽॽउपरहरोॽदॽपाॽशाॽेगॽ
ॽॽहरमेहरॽबोॽधॽॽ

MS Indien 722 Folio 19, Bibliothèque nationale, Paris

Throughout the centuries Gaush Urva was held in great love and reverence by devout Zoroastraians. She was revered by Parsi and Irani Zoroastrians who came to India as refugees in the tenth and mid nineteenth centuries respectively.

She is also sketched in an unpublished manuscript and depicted as an Elamite figurine (See illustrations).

In the Bibliotheque Nationale, Paris, is an 18th century manuscript, *MS Indien 722*, which is a version of the *Arda Viraf Nama*[8] written by hand, in old Gujarati, by an anonymous Parsi priest of Bombay. The lettering is feeble, and the grammar not always correct. What causes confusion is the horizontal line above each letter which is the practice in Sanskrit and Hindi, but not in Gujarati.

Folio 19 has a delightful sketch of Gaush Urva. She is shown as a beautiful, young cow, smiling, with one leg raised as if about to dance. She stands on a box containing what appear to be nine Barsom twigs.[9] The halter of servitude is round her neck. Below her is a pool showing tiny wavelets, the whole surrounded by a border of fishes, nose to tail. Interspersed between the sketch and the lettering, is a profusion of stylised flowers and flying birds.

Facing Gaush Urva is a male figure, standing. In his right hand he holds a palm leaf with a long stem. Behind him is a palm tree with five feathery palms. He is clothed in the priestly robes of *jama-pichhori* and wears a Mogul turban on his head. His left arm is bent at the elbow and his fingers are clenched, holding, possibly, a pinch of incense to be dropped on the Sacred Fire.

The Sacred Fire is in the centre of the page, in an **Afarghan** or Fire Censer, which is placed on a tripod with its three steps representing the motto of the religion: **Humata**, Good Thoughts, **Hukhta**, Good words, **Huvarashta**, Good Deeds. Above the leaping flames, is the Bell which is rung when the **Boi**[10] ceremony is performed by the priest, at the changing of each of the five **Gahs** viz. Havan Gah, from dawn to noon; Rapithwan Gah, from noon till 3 p.m., Uziren from 3 p.m. to sunset: Aiwisuthrem from sunset till midnight, and Ushain from midnight till dawn.

Behind Gaush Urva is a plant with nine flowers and leaves, the whole inclining gracefully across the page.

To the left of Gaush Urva is another male figure, seated, clothed in *achkan* and *churidar pyjama* typically Mogul. He also wears a Mogul turban. His left arm is bent at the elbow, the hand clutching a triangular object. This could be a wine glass or the triangular wedge of the **Dron**,[11] the sacred, unleavened bread which is blest and later partaken of by priest and laity present at the ceremony. The seated figure would seem to be Shah Ardeshir (Papakan) of the text.

The script explains the drawing. Here is my translation of the Gujarati lettering:

> "The Shah knew the meaning of the Avesta. That man,
> reading the Zend Avesta with the intense heat of his
> mind (lit. boiling heat), and with a relaxed body,
> discovered (its true meaning). With this (Fire in his
> mind) Ardeshir Padshah built the Dar-e-Meher."

Elamite Figurine
in silver.
Metropolitan
Museum of Art,
Joseph Pulitzer
Bequest, 1966.
(66.173)

We now realise that the drawing represents the Yasna
ceremony performed in the royal households of ancient Iranian
kings at dawn to consecrate the Dron or unleavened bread, and
the wine, before any member could place a morsel of food or drink
in his mouth. All the four elements are represented by their
symbols. The priest stands on the Earth. Fire is in the Fire Censer.
Water is represented by the wavelets and the fish border. Air
surrounds all, including Gaush Urva who represents the animal
kingdom. Plants are present in the palm tree, the flowering branch
and in the decorative flowers strewn in the background. The fact
that Gaush Urva stands on nine symbolic barsom twigs indicates
that the ceremony is being performed in a royal household,
especially as Ardeshir Padshah is present. The author of the
Nirangistan[12] informs us that nine barsom twigs are necessary for
this royal consecration.

This page has been reproduced without comment in Jean Varenne's delightful little book *Zarathushtra et la tradition mazdéenne,* Series Maîtres spirituels, Ed. Seuil, Paris, 1966, p. 122.

It is also reproduced in Mohammad Mokhri's learned study, *La Lumière et le Feu dans l'Iran ancien*, Leuven, 2nd. ed. 1982, p. 81, with passing comments on the sacred Fire and the mistaken assumption that both male figures represent Zoroastrian priests.

Gaush Urva is also depicted as mentioned earlier, in an Elamite, silver figurine, about three inches high, housed in the Metropolitan Museum of Art, New York.[13] She is seated on her knees, holding a large karafe in her front hoofs. It seems she is offering a libation, perhaps her own milk. She wears a striped skirt with a tiny design between the stripes. One of her ears is pierced and a large ring inserted therein, again a symbol of her servitude to man. She looks a pathetic little figure pleading for protection in return for the libation she is offering.

Both Mary Boyce and J. Duchesne-Guillemin point out that the myth of Gaush Urva has "come down to us from very ancient times in diverse forms in India, Georgia, and in the Book of Enoch in a Slavonic Version" (Duchesne-Guillemin *art.cit.* p. 9).

Gaush Tasha:

Closely associated with Gaush Urva is **Gaush Tasha**, the Shaper of the Cow or Creator of Cattle. In *Yasna* 29, when Gaush Urva complains of the brutality practised upon her by mankind, then it is Gaush Tasha who approaches Truth and inquires as to who he will appoint to protect her (Ys.29.2).
Gaush Tasha is next referred to in Ys.31.9:

"O Ahura Mazda,
   since to You belongs Devotion
   to You the Creator of Cattle,
   and to You the dynamism of the Spirit,
   therefore you gave her (the Cow),
   the choice of a way,

either to stay with the caring herdsman
or with him who never was one." (Ys.31.9)

Again, Gaush Tasha is mentioned:

"Whatever is Yours through Truth,
Whatever the Creator of Cattle, Gaush Tasha,
has declared to Truth,
with these all men will question me through
the Good Mind". (Ys.46.9)

These are the only three references to Gaush Tasha in the
Gathas. It is not clear what exactly is the function of this symbol.

Twin Mentalities:

Zarathushtra, however, has yet to explain to his listeners
how Evil came into the World. He does so in Yasna 30.1–11 and 45.2.
Again, as in the Legend of Gaush Urva, he makes use of an ancient
parable concerning the Twin Mainyu, or Mentalities, whom he
describes as "vahyo" the "better" and "akem" the evil mentality.
These two are in opposition to each other in thought, word and
deed. Man has to choose between these two. Zarathushtra is
unique in insisting that each individual choose between these two
tendencies and so be fully responsible for his actions.

"Listen to the noblest teachings
with an attentive ear.
With your penetrating mind discriminate
between these twin mentalities,
man by man, each one for his own self.
Awake, to proclaim this Truth
before the Final Judgment overtakes you." (Ys.30.2)

He then proceeds to explain the parable. In the beginning,
that is, when Time began, the Twins revealed themselves in vision
and established "gaya" or mortal life, and "ajyaiti," non-life.

The wise and the generous chose correctly between these

two, but the unwise and mean did not. Now the Evil Mentality elected to perform the worst deeds, but the Most Bountiful Spirit who dwells in imperishable Light chose Truth. And so did those who rejoiced Ahura Mazda by their actions. The false gods Daevas, and their worshippers, did not discriminate between these two. Confusion came upon them as they debated, and so they chose the Worst Mind. Straightaway, they fell headlong into Wrath, and so poisoned not only the life of mankind, but the whole of existence.

The sincere individual, however, is not left helpless. Ahura Mazda's Sovereignty comes to his aid through the Good Mind and Truth, while compassionate Devotion bestows upon him "the sustaining breath of life" (Ys.30.7).

Retribution, however, overtakes those who choose wrongly. It is then that Ahura Mazda's Truth and Good Mind ensure the Sovereignty to "those who deliver the Lie into the hands of Truth" (Ys.30.8). The Lie and the Truth cannot exist within each other. Truth will absorb the Lie and annihilate it. Zarathushtra therefore asks: "How shall I deliver the Lie into the hands of Truth to destroy it completely through the Sacred Words of Your Teaching?" (Ys.44.14). The Power and prosperity of the wicked will also be destroyed. At the same time, the Truth-seekers will share in the promised reward and "dwell with the Good Mind, Truth and Wisdom" (Ys.30.10). This chapter concludes with the following assurance to all mankind:

> "So understand, O mortal men, the Decrees
> which Mazda has established regarding happiness and
> misery.
> There will be
> a long period of suffering for the wicked,
> and salvation for the just,
> but thereafter
> eternal bliss shall prevail everywhere."   (Ys.30.11)

Life becomes a battleground between the Ashavans, the Seekers after Truth, and the Dregvants, Worshippers of Falsehood, the Druj, the Lie.

As the responsibility for choice rests on every man, Zarathushtra now describes the inborn faculties through which he can discriminate between the true and the false.

Inborn Faculties:

"O Mazda, from the beginning
    You fashioned for us
    physical bodies, an awakened conscience and a
    directive intelligence
    through Your own Mind.
    You infused life breath
    into mortal forms.
    You granted us
    capacities to act and true teachings to guide us.
    so that we could choose to be with You or against You."
                                                    (Ys.31.11)

"Since then
    each lifts up his voice to proclaim his faith,
    both the liar and the truth-speaker,
    whether learned or unlearned,
    according to his own heart and mind.
    But compassionate Devotion stands by
    to deliberate with the spirit
    of whoever is perplexed by doubt."   (Ys.31.12)

Sraosha:

Besides the above faculties, man also has **Sraosha** to guide him. Sraosha is derived from the root, "sru" inward hearing, the capacity to be still and "hearken" to the voice of Ahura Mazda within us. Sraosha is always accompanied by **Ashi Vanghui,** Ashi the good, Ashi the blest. She represents both the material and spiritual wealth which comes to anyone who dedicates himself to Ahura Mazda, i.e. to Life and Wisdom. She is often mentioned in the Gathas. It is Sraosha who comes laden with "radiant rewards" (*rayo Ashish*) to be distributed among the Truth-seekers and the Worshippers of Falsehood. But to the latter these "rewards" are the bitter, foul smelling food of their own thoughts and acts. (Ys.31.20)

There are two other faculties in Man which help him to choose right. These are **Khratu** and **Chisti**. The word Khratu is also found in the Vedas where it means "force" or "energy." Zarathushtra gives the word his own particular meaning.

Khratu:

Khratu in the Gathas signifies mental energy, a directive intelligence with which man plans his work. When associated with the Good Mind or with Ahura Mazda, Khratu signifies wisdom, Hu-Khratu, the Good Khratu, as in Ys.28.1 and 45.6. But there is a Dush-Khratu, an Evil Intellect, which plans death and destruction through the acts of wicked men (Ys.32.14;48.10;49.4). Khratu also denotes the Will or Purpose of Ahura Mazda for His Creation (Ys.32.4; 32.14; 43.6; 49.6).

Chisti:

The close companion of the Good Khratu, Hu-Khratu, is **Chisti**, feminine in gender and derived from the root, "chi" to penetrate deeply. Chisti in the Gathas signifies luminous insight leading to enlightenment. Zarathushtra prays for good rulers to rule through actions inspired by Hu-Chisti, the Good Chisti (Ys.48.5). It is "oya Chisti," unique insight, which makes man realise that Ahura Mazda is the "Father of Truth" (Ys.47.2). Every individual's **Daena**, or conscience, grows in Truth through his Chisti (Ys.51.21). To lead man "along the paths of the Good Chisti" means to prepare the way for enlightenment (Ys.46.4).[14]

Manthra:

Intelligence and insight are essential to the understanding of another basic concept in the Gathas, the **Manthra**, (Vedic *mantra*), the Sacred Word of Power. In Hinduism there are literally hundreds of mantras for every conceivable occasion in life. The Vedic *mantra* is derived from the root, "man" to think, and the syllable "tra" meaning that which guides and protects. So the Vedic mantra means that which guides and protects the mind. Zarathushtra declares his Manthra to be "the greatest of all truths," (Ys.28.5), because it emanates from Truth, that is, from Ahura Mazda Himself, and is to be spread among mankind through his Sovereignty. (Ys.28.7; 44.17).

Zarathushtra's definition of the Manthra makes it a World Manthra to be acted upon by every man in his daily life.(Ys.31.6; 45.3 and 5). Zarathushtra describes himself as a **Manthran**, a Preacher of the Manthra (Ys.50.5). This word is found in the **Sengha**, or Sacred Teachings. No wonder the older generation of Zoroastrians described their religious books as "Manthra-vani," the "food" of the Manthra. As one would expect, the Manthra is related to Perfection and Immortality who "dwell in the dazzling light" of Ahura Mazda's Wisdom, (Ys.33.9). The Worshippers of Falsehood, however, compose their own "evil incantations" to persuade others to join them in delivering "the home, the town, the province and the country to strife and destruction"(Ys.31.18).

In preaching his conception of the World Manthra, Zarathushtra makes use of two pre-Gathic symbols familiar to both the initiate and the learned in his audience as well as to the herdsman. These symbols are: **Hvare Kshaeta**, the Resplendent Sun, and **Atash Khoreh**, the Glorious Fire.

Sun:

In the Gathas, the Sun is the symbol of Truth and Wisdom. Ahura Mazda is the close companion of the Sun of Truth (Ys.32.2), while those who follow Truth also behold the Sun of Wisdom (Ys.50.2). The light of the Sun is precious in the eyes of the Good Mind (Ys.50.10), while the "glittering dawning of the days" exist for Ahura Mazda's praise and adoration through Truth (Ys.46.3). These "bright sunrisings" also herald the coming of the "Saviours of the lands," the Saoshyants, who are destined to be the "destroyers of Wrath"(Ys.48.12).

Fire:

Atar or Fire, plays a key role in the Gathas even as *Agni*
(Fire) does in the Vedas. Atar represents the Fire of Thought both
in Ahura Mazda and in the mind of Man. Zarathushtra appeals to
all men to "live in harmony with Truth" and then explains what he
means:

> "O Ahura, You offer that harmony
> to each of these two contenders
> by means of Your hidden Fire and Truth
> in keeping with Your Decrees.
> O Mazda,
> with Your very own mouth and tongue
> proclaim this to us
> for our enlightenment. . . ." (Ys.31.3)

He further adds:

> "Therefore, O Ahura,
> we long for Your Fire,
> mighty through Truth.
> This enduring flame is offered to the true believer
> for his support.
> But for the destruction loving,
> this raging flame will scorch him
> with just a turn of the hand." (Ys.34.4)

In other words, the Lie is burnt up by Truth. Moreover,
Zarathushtra associates Fire with Thought in the Mind of man. In a
verse incorporated in the prayers which accompany the daily
ritual of the tying and untying of the sacred thread, the *Kushti*,
worn around the waist by all devout Zoroastrians, Zarathushtra
asserts:

> "O Mazda,
> whom have You appointed as protector over me
> when the Follower of the Lie threatens me with violence?
> Who other than Your Fire

and Your Mind through whose actions Truth is fulfilled
O Ahura? . . ."   (Ys.46.7)

Zarathushtra goes even further by associating Fire with
Spenta Mainyu, the Spirit of Benediction:

"O Mazda Ahura,
You distribute their just dues to the two contenders
through Your Spirit of Benediction
and Your Fire.
This shall indeed
convert the many who are seekers
sustained by Devotion and Truth."   (Ys.47.6)

Physical Fire, therefore, becomes an emblem of the divine
once it has been consecrated. Hence, the Fire in Zoroastrian
Temples burns night and day. No Zoroastrian ceremony can be
performed without the presence of Fire, even if it be but a tiny,
lighted wick *(divo)* floating in a glass of oil, for Fire is witness to
the Truth. In Vedic ceremonies also, Fire as witness, *Agni shakshi,*
is always present.

Maga:

Besides Fire and the Sun, another key concept in the
Gathas is **Maga**, or the Sacramental Gift Exchange. The word,
Maga, has undergone many different interpretations ever since the
Gathas have been studied critically. Today, scholars feel that maga
signifies a sacrament, specially a sacramental gift exchange
between Man and Ahura Mazda. The word occurs for the first time
in *Yasna* 29.11. After Gaush Urva is reconciled to Zarathushtra as
her deliverer he appeals to everyone to accept the new teaching
offered by Ahura Mazda as a sacramental duty, for this teaching
will bring man enlightenment. We next come across the word,
maga, in the controversial verse, *Yasna* 44.18. Zarathushtra offers
all his worldly wealth consisting of ten mares, a stallion, and a
camel, in exchange for Perfection and Immortality. Zarathushtra is
poor. He confesses he owns very few animals and his followers are
few (Ys.46.2). Yet in utter sincerity he makes the offering realising

that Ahura Mazda, out of His Bounty, will bless him with the
unsurpassed gifts of Perfection and Immortality.

Again, the Prophet praises his ally, the "valiant Kavi
Vishtaspa" for "taking part in the great sacramental gift exchange,"
(Ys.46.14). He further inquires who among his followers "strives
after the sacramental gift of the Good Mind" (Ys.51.11). He promises
his followers Heaven or the House of Song, as a reward "to those
sharing the sacramental gift exchange" (Ys.51.15). Once again, he
praises Kavi Vishtaspa for attaining enlightenment "through the
power of the sacrament" (Ys.51.16). Finally, in the last Gatha which
celebrates the marriage of his daughter, Pouruchista, married
couples are urged to love one another through Truth and consider
this a sacramental duty or else "at the last gasp"their cry will be
"Woe" (Ys.53.7).

As Zarathushtra divided the world into the **Ashavans**,
followers of Truth, and the **Dregvants**, Worshippers of Falsehood,
the concepts of rewards and punishments, Heaven and Hell came
into existence. In Zoroastrianism these are mental states, not
physical locations.

Heaven:

Heaven is **Garo Demana**, the House of Song, the House of
Bliss or Ushta. Zarathushtra offers his prayers and those of his
followers to be "treasured" in Ahura Mazda's House of Song
(Ys.45.8). The Seeker after Truth is firmly set upon his path by
"listening to the voice of Sraosha which leads those worthy to the
House of Song" (Ys.50.4). Ahura Mazda is said to be the "first" to
enter the House of Song. Man has to earn the privilege of entering
this blissful state of mind by following his own Good Mind and
Truth which will lead to his salvation and to the House of Song.

Hell:

Hell or **Drujo-Demana**, the House of the Lie, is a state of
mental anguish suffered by wicked souls. This state is described
in picturesque imagery by the Prophet.

"Whoever clings to the Followers of Truth,
 his dwelling shall be the Light.
 But for you,
 O Worshippers of Falsehood,
 a long life of darkness, foul food and woeful wailings—
 to such an existence
 will your evil conscience
 lead you through your own deeds."   (Ys.31.20)

Chinvat: Bridge of Judgement

As the Kavis (princelings) and the Karapans (mumbler priests) are both corrupt and have yoked mankind "to the destruction of life," their souls and evil conscience will torment them when they reach the Bridge of Judgment. They will remain in the House of the Lie till the end of Time (Ys.46.11). The Karapans specially have condemned themselves to be placed in the House of the Lie because of "their injury to the herd by their actions and beliefs": (Ys.51.14). Zarathushtra has a penetrating psychological insight into the mental condition of the wicked:

"The conscience of the wicked man
 destroys for himself the reality of Truth.
 His soul shall torment him with retributive vengeance
 at the Bridge of the Separator, the Bridge of Judgement,
 for his own deeds and his tongue strayed
 from the path of Truth."   (Ys.51.13)

Every time we make a decision in this life, based on choice, we are crossing the Chinvato pérétu, the Bridge of the Separator, separating the good from the evil.

Later tradition, however, asserts that both the just and the unjust will have to be purified by passing through rivers of red-hot molten metal before the **Frashokéréti,** the Renewal of Existence, can be established. To the just, this will seem like walking through "warm milk" but not so to the unjust.

Zarathushtra boldly exclaims: "Forth with them all (man or woman) I will cross the Bridge of Judgment" (Ys.46.10).

A different view of the Final Judgment is also found in the Gathas. Zarathushtra announces that "at the last turning point of existence" Ahura Mazda will come accompanied by His Spirit of Benediction, His Sovereignty and with His Good Mind through whom living beings progress in the Truth. Armaiti will then instruct all souls in the purpose of Ahura Mazda's Wisdom (Ys.43.6). The inference seems to be that each soul will be taught to develop his/her faculties and learn to live fully in a different dimension of existence from that of the earthly.

Sava:

Sava or Salvation is offered to all by Ahura Mazda: "Indeed, all those who are, who were, who shall be long for the Salvation He offers" (Ys.45.7). The corrupt princes and priests, however, reject the offer:

"When O Mazda,
will men recognise the message of Salvation?

When will they remove this filth of a drink
by which these hostile Karapans, through their
perverse intellect,
cause intoxication and so delude the evil rulers of
these lands?" (Ys.48.10).[15]

Ahura Mazda dwells in the "straight paths of salvation"
(Ys.43.3) and appoints a caring husbandsman for the salvation of
the world (Ys.29.6). He holds Salvation and Dissolution in the same
hand (Ys.43.4), for what redeems the just, destroys the wicked
(Ys.43.12). He has pledged Salvation to the Followers of Truth
(Ys.51.9), so Zarathushtra prays that the blessings of Ahura Mazda's
Salvation may come to him through the Good Mind (Ys.51.2).

Saoshyants:

To hasten the process of Salvation, Zarathushtra conceives
the idea of the **Saoshyants**, the "Saviours of the lands" (Ys.48.12).
They are inspired by Truth and destined to be the "destroyers of
Wrath" (Ys.34.13; 48.12). They will guide mankind towards the
"Truth-inspired existence" and herald the dawning of a new day
(Ys.46.3). Ahura Mazda Himself has laid out "the straight paths of
the Religion" for the Saoshyants to follow (Ys.53.2). Later tradition
introduces a particular saviour, **Saoshyos**, who will appear at the
end of time and bring about the Frashokéréti.

In the Gathas, no particular Saviour is mentioned who will
redeem the world. The Saoshyants are all righteous men and
women who work to establish Truth and Justice in the World,
avoiding Wrath and bloodshed. Again, we are told that the "Truth
inspired existence" will be upheld by the guiding intellect of the
Saviours. (Ys.46.3).

Frashokéréti:

Zarathushtra is very conscious of his mission on earth, yet
the word, Frashokéréti, the total transformation of Man and
Society towards which he worked, is not mentioned in the Gathas.
Instead, there are various references to this future event. In his

intimate communings with Ahura Mazda he begs for "knowledge of the long-continued, desired existence which none can compel from You, and which is said to lie in Your Sovereignty" (Ys.43.13). In the beautiful chapter on Questionings, Zarathushtra asks:

> "Does the wondrous Renewal of Life yet to come bring
>   the best reward of Salvation upon the ardent devotee ?"
>
> (Ys.44.2)

Once more Zarathushtra questions:

> "When will the just overcome the wicked, O Mazda?
> Then indeed
> will come about the wondrous renewal of life."   (Ys.48.2)

Hamkar:

Closely connected with the Frashokéréti is Zarathushtra's idea of the **Hamkar**, fellow-worker, a concept not found in other religions. The prophet insists that every man must become a hamkar with Ahura Mazda and together they will strive to establish the blissful Renewal of Existence. Never before in the history of religion had man been invited to hold such an exalted position.

This togetherness is further emphasized by the **Hamazor**, or spiritual handclasp. On auspicious days like Nau Roze, or New Year's Day, priests in the Fire Temples form a circle before the Sacred Fire. They cross their arms, their right hand clasping the left of their neighbour while their left clasps the right of the neighbour. A formula of greeting is recited:

> *"Hamazor hama Asho bède . . ."*
> May you be righteous. May you live long.

What helps an individual to make intelligent choices in his/her every day life? Surely it is to understand the nature of Ahura Mazda and His Powers, for these dwell in everyone.

Ahura-Mazda's First Thought blazed into myriads of sparks of light. (Ys.31.7)

Ahura Mazda:

Let us begin with **Ahura Mazda** who is Life and Wisdom. Zarathushtra describes Him as the "First and the Last for all Eternity, as the Father of Good Mind, the true Creator of Truth, and Lord over the actions of life" (Ys.31.8). His "daughter" is Armaiti, "Nourisher of good deeds." Not to be deceived is the all-seeing Ahura. He is "Vispanam Datarem," Creator of all, (Ys.44.7); Hu-Dao, Giver of all good, (Ys.48.3); Data Angheush, Creator of Life, (Ys.50.11); He is Spenishta Mainyu Mazda, Most Bountiful Spirit, Mazda (Ys.33.12;43.2;51.7), worthy to be loved, radiant in action, Lord of Life and Truth (Ys.46.9). He is supremely just, eternally the same, the Mighty and Most Bountiful One (Ys.43.4), who pours out His blessing on every thing that lives (Ys.45.6). At the "last turning point of existence" He will come with His Spirit of Benediction, his Sovereignty, His Good Mind and Devotion to help the Soul after death (Ys.43.6). He holds Salvation and Dissolution in "the same hand" (Ys.43.4) to be distributed among the Ashavans the Truth-seekers, and the Dregvants, Worshippers of Falsehood. He has established His Decrees regarding happiness and misery. A long period of suffering will come to the wicked, and salvation to the just, but thereafter "eternal bliss shall prevail everywhere" (Ys.30.11).

Man and the Universe are governed by Ahura Mazda through His six special Powers which emanate from Him, the first two being **Asha**, Truth, Justice, the Cosmic Order; and **Vohu Mana,** the Good Mind. This last is a unique conception in the history of religions. But first, let us try to understand Asha.

Asha:

Asha, Cosmic Order, Truth, "is given us for our choice, the support of our faith, and the destruction of wickedness" (Ys.49.3). Truth is also "the heritage of all, the guardian in spirit, the healer of life, the friend" (Ys.44.2). Ahura Mazda and Truth are one (Ys.28.8; 29.7). It is Ahura Mazda's Truth which leads all men into "the light" of enlightenment (Ys.28.2). Zarathushtra's teaching will spread in the world through Truth and the Sovereignty of Ahura

Mazda (Ys.32.6), for the Prophet walks along the straight paths of
Truth where Ahura Mazda Himself dwells (Ys.33.5). It is Truth which
fosters human life (Ys.33.11), which is fulfilled through the "actions"
of Ahura Mazda's Fire and His Mind (Ys.46.7). This means that every
man must think for himself and work his way to the Truth by
exercising the "fire of thought" deep within him. Hence, physical
fire is considered a victorious emblem of Truth, and as such is
consecrated in Zoroastrian Fire Temples. The Twin Powers,
Perfection and Immortality, are the constant companions of Truth
(Ys.33.9). All his earthly life, man should strive to attain these divine
gifts.

Vohu Mana:

Vohu Mana, the Good Mind, is closely associated with
Truth. Several types of mind are mentioned in the Gathas. There is
Mana or manangha, mind, from which thought proceeds (Ys.46.7).
There is also Vohu Mana, the Good Mind, and **Ako Mana,** the Evil
Mind. Man has the choice to think good thoughts or evil thoughts
for both proceed out of Mind (Ys.30.3). Vahishta Mana, Supreme
Mind is an attribute solely of Ahura Mazda, just as Spenishta
Mainyu, the Most Benevolent Spirit, is His alone. Truth and Good
Mind, however, are His two most active Powers who help men and
women to choose the right and just actions in life. These two
ensure the Sovereignty to those who "deliver the Lie into the hands
of Truth" (Ys.30.8). The Truth and the Lie cannot exist in one and the
same faculty. Truth absorbs the Lie and destroys it (Ys.44.14).
Zarathushtra prays that he may reach Ahura Mazda "in fullness of
knowledge that comes from the Good Mind" (Ys.28.2). He addresses
Truth and the Good Mind as if they were his personal friends:
"Truth , when shall I see you? And you, O Good Mind, ripe in
wisdom?" (Ys.28.5). He speaks to Ahura Mazda in these moving
words: "Come, Spirit of Eternal Life, come, O Ahura, with the Good
Mind and bless us with Your Truth's everlasting gifts. . . ." (Ys.28.6).

It is to the Good Mind that Gaush Urva turns in her distress
"O Good Mind, whom have you proclaimed as protector over me
and my herds before all mankind?" (Ys.29.7). Then she prays to
Ahura Mazda to grant Zarathushtra and his followers "eminence

and Sovereignty through Truth" and hopes they will establish "a
peaceful and happy existence through the Good Mind" (Ys.29.10).
When the prosperity of the wicked is destroyed, then the
followers of good will share in the promised reward and "dwell
with the Good Mind, Truth and Wisdom." (Ys.30.10).

The Good Mind plays a leading role in the sublime Gatha of
Enlightenment, the *Ushtavaiti, Yasna* 43. As for example:

"When the full force of the Good Mind took possession of
me,
O Mazda,
then I realised You as Mighty and Bountiful. . . ."   (Ys.43.4)

Zarathushtra implores Ahura Mazda for "that radiant
reward" the "life of the Good Mind" (Ys.43.1). He prays that all
mankind may enjoy "unlimited bliss."

"By means of Truth and Your Most Bountiful Spirit,
grant O Mazda, enlightenment
and the full measure of the Good Mind
so that each may enjoy unlimited bliss
all the days of his long life."   (Ys.43.2)

The Good Mind encourages Zarathushtra to ask deep and
searching questions, which he does. These lead to his
enlightenment:

". . . When I first became enlightened through Your
inspired words,
then I realised
that to do what is best for mankind
would cause me suffering."   (Ys. 43.11)

"Then You said to me:
"Go, instruct mankind in the Truth,
and reveal teachings hitherto unheard of.
Hasten towards my Sraosha, laden with radiant rewards."
                                                        (Ys.43.12)

It is the Good Mind who declares to Zarathushtra that "silent meditation **(Tushnamaiti)** is best for man" (Ys.43.15). This chapter ends with a profound verse:

"Thus, O Ahura,
Zarathushtra chooses for himself the Most Bountiful
Spirit which is Yours.
May Truth incarnate through the power of the life-
breath.
May Devotion ever abide with Sovereignty
in sun-like splendour.
May she shower blessings
upon deeds inspired by the Good Mind." (Ys.43.16)

Khashathra:

Khashathra, Ahura Mazda's Sovereignty, his Might and Majesty, His Kingdom, His Power, is mentioned no less than thirty-seven times in the Gathas. This Power is closely linked with Truth and the Good Mind. In the very first chapter of the Gathas, Zarathushtra requests Ahura Mazda to grant His Sovereignty for the salvation of man (Ys.28.9), while Gaush Urva begs Ahura Mazda to grant Zarathushtra and his followers eminence and Sovereignty through Truth (Ys.29.10). The Lie will be conquered through Ahura Mazda's Sovereignty (Ys.31.4), while those who deliver the Lie into the hands of Truth will receive His Sovereignty through Truth and the Good Mind (Ys.30.8). The wise counsellor seeks to further Sovereignty in the home, the province and the country because he upholds Truth and Sovereignty in his every word and deed (Ys.31.16 and 22).

Thus the true doctrine will be spread among mankind through Ahura Mazda's Truth and Sovereignty (Ys.32.6). Zarathushtra gains "the long-lasting Sovereignty of the Good Mind" by walking "along the straight paths of Truth where Ahura Mazda dwells" (Ys.33.5). It is He who nourishes the Good Mind and Sovereignty for the fabulous gifts of that Sovereignty are the blessings of the Good Mind (Ys.33.11).

Ahura Mazda grants man Immortality, Truth and His Sovereignty which flows from Perfection and is inherent in the Good Mind (Ys.34.1 and 11). At the "last turning point of existence" He will come with His Spirit of Benediction, His Sovereignty and the Good Mind through whom living beings progress in Truth (Ys.43.6).

Zarathushtra wants to attain glory through Ahura Mazda's Sovereignty (Ys.43.8), but this Sovereignty can only be obtained by asking Ahura Mazda "searching questions" through which Zarathushtra will gain understanding (Ys.43.10). He yearns for the knowledge of the long-continued, desired existence (the Frashokéréti) which is said to be Ahura Mazda's Sovereignty (Ys.43.13). Zarathushtra places the souls of the just together with the Good Mind and his homage to Armaiti, Devotion, in the House of Song and requests Ahura Mazda to strengthen them through His Sovereignty (Ys.49.10). Moreover, Wisdom, Truth, the Good Mind and the promised Sovereignty will come to "those who behold the Sun of Wisdom" for Zarathushtra praises Ahura Mazda through these Powers (Ys.50.2 and 4). In the last verse of the Gathas Zarathushtra complains bitterly that corruption fastens upon those of evil choice who attempt to annihilate the right living. He cries out in anguish:

> "Where is the Lord of Justice
> who would deprive them of life and volition?
> That, O Mazda is Your Sovereignty
> by which You grant the greater Glory
> to the upright Drighu (the oppressed and the forsaken
> crying out for justice)."   (Ys.53.9)

Armaiti:

Armaiti (lit. Right-mindedness), Devotion is the opposite of Taromaiti, wrong-headedness, cussedness. She is also the opposite of Pairimaiti, devious, roundabout reasoning. Zarathushtra links Armaiti with Tushnamaiti, silent, meditative thought. Armaiti symbolises Devotion, Love, Piety and Zeal.

She is the most gracious of Ahura Mazda's Powers, His "very own Beloved". She is also the "Beloved of the Wise" and the "Treasured One of the Good mind" (Ys.48.6). It is she who bestows upon man "the sustaining breath of life" (Ys.30.7), and comes to the rescue of those perplexed by doubts (Ys.31.12). Twice she is called Ahura Mazda's "daughter" whom he brings with Him when Zarathushtra is invited to place before them his searching questions by which he will attain enlightenment (Ys.43.10; Cf.Ys.45.4). She is the "nourisher of good deeds" and furthers Truth by inspiring the words and deeds of good men.

She illumines the conscience in man through Truth (Ys.33.13) and is intimately connected with that Power as we see in the following verse:

"O Frashaoshtra Hvogva,
come, join the faithful
with those for whom we both wish this life's blessings:
blessings where Perfect Devotion blends with Truth,
where the desirable Kingdom of the Good Mind is found,
where the Lord of Life and Wisdom abides

in the Heaven of His Bounty.   (Ys.46.16)

Moreover, the best life will be cultivated by him who "speaks with words from the mouth and tongue of the Good Mind" and whose actions "are performed by the hands of Devotion" (Ys.47.2) whose "inspired words" lead him to act justly (Ys.44.10). It is she who brings to the caring herdsman the "peace of Devotion" so that he may take counsel with the Good Mind (Ys.47.3).

Zarathushtra appeals directly to Armaiti to let " good rulers rule over us. Let not wicked rulers rule over us" (Ys.48.5). A few verses further, Zarathushtra asks:

"When, O Mazda,
    will your loving Devotion, Armaiti,
    in harmony with Truth,
    give us good shelter and rich pasturage through Your
    Sovereignty?"   (Ys.48.11)

Armaiti, therefore becomes the genius of the Earth. Later tradition faithfully reflects this Gathic view by asserting that her mantle is the star-studded Sky, for the Sky covers the Earth. Zarathushtra further declares: " Silent meditation (Tushnamaiti) is best for man" (Ys.43.15). Pahlavi writers explain Tushnamaiti as "Silent, meditative thought " and Armaiti as "perfect thought" in the mind of man (*Dinkart*, Bk IX, chap. 43).

Dastur M.N. Dhalla, in his *Zoroastrian Theology*, explains the true significance of Armaiti. He writes:
"Vohu Manah teaches man to know Ahura Mazda, Armaiti inspires him to love the Lord . . . Devotion is the first requisite. Mere muttering of a few formulas with the lips is no prayer. Where there is no such prayer, there is no devotion; and where there is no devotion, there is no religion."[16]

Armaiti's intrinsic nature is perfectly enshrined in a legend ascribed to Zarathushtra by Pahlavi writers and which was well known in Sasanian times. Here is a rendering of the text:

"O Ahura Mazda, Spirit Most Holy, who is that being seated beside You? Her one hand is round Your neck, the other clings to Your hand. Her eyes never leave Yours, nor do Yours leave hers. Who is she?" Ahura Mazda replied: She is Spendarmat (Spenta Armaiti), My daughter, the mistress of My House (of Song, Paradise), and the mother of all creatures.[17]

Armaiti is the golden thread that draws all the other Powers together, for, without Love and Devotion the universe could not exist except as an empty shell.

Haurvatat and Ameretat:

The last two of **Ahura Mazda's** special Powers are **Haurvatat**, Health, Well-being, Perfection; and **Ameretat,** Immortality. They are described as twins who live "in the dazzling light" of Ahura Mazda's Wisdom (Ys.33.9). They are the rewards the individual earns by following Truth. The initiate will receive "the best" by spreading Ahura Mazda's "true and Sacred Word relating to Perfection, Immortality and Truth" (Ys.31.6) while Zarathushtra prays his speech may "grow in power to reach up to Perfection and Immortality through the Sacred Word the Manthra, which emanates from Truth" (Ys.44.17).

These Twin Powers nourish the Soul in man (Ys.34.11) and because of his righteous actions, Ahura Mazda blesses man with "Immortality, Truth, and the Sovereignty which flows from Perfection" (Ys.34.1). Ahura Mazda announces: "My Word is best for mortals to hear. They who will offer willing obedience to My Word will advance towards Perfection and Immortality" (Ys.45.5). Hence, the souls of the just dwell in Immortality (Ys.45.7) while Ahura Mazda assigns to man Perfection and Immortality in His Kingdom through Truth and the Good Mind (Ys.45.10).

Zarathushtra offers all his meagre wealth to Ahura Mazda in exchange for the gifts of Perfection and Immortality (Ys.44.18). It is, however, in the opening verse of the chapter dedicated to Spenta Mainyu, Ahura Mazda's Spirit of Benediction, that all the Powers are mentioned together, indicating their subtle interrelationships:

> "Through Your Spirit of Benediction,
> and Your Supreme Mind,
> You will grant Perfection and Immortality to him
> whose words and deeds are in harmony with Truth,
> with the Sovereignty of Mazda
> and the Devotion of Ahura."   (Ys.47.1)

Zarathushtra begs Ahura Mazda to guide his work so that he may worship Him through the Good Mind and Truth, thus earning for himself and his followers the twin rewards of Perfection and Immortality (Ys.33.8). Once again Zarathushtra begs for these through Ahura Mazda's Most Bountiful Spirit (Ys.51.7). A good Zoroastrian, therefore, prays for a long life on earth to fight Evil till his dying breath and so earn Perfection and Immortality.

The value of the Gathas lies in the teachings they embody. Before we turn to them it might be advisable to review briefly what Zarathushtra considers his mission to be.

In the opening verse of the Gathas, he prays for the abiding support of Ahura Mazda's ever-expanding Spirit of Benediction. He pledges all his actions to Truth. He seeks the wisdom of the Good Mind to guide him so that he may gladden Gaush Urva (Ys.28.1). Here she symbolises not only cattle but also the voice of the oppressed and the forsaken crying out for justice. In the very next chapter, *Yasna* 29, we learn that Ahura Mazda has appointed Zarathushtra as the protecting herdsman of Gaush Urva who is so brutally treated by mankind (Ys.29.1 and 6). *Yasna* 29 concludes with Zarathushtra invoking Truth, the Good Mind and the Sovereignty of Ahura Mazda and appealing to all men to "accept the new teaching of enlightenment offered by Mazda as a sacramental duty" (Ys.29.11).

After explaining the origin of Evil, he begins to preach concerning the sacred Decrees Ahura Mazda offers both to the Seekers after Truth and the Worshippers of Falsehood. He then boldly announces his mission before an audience of powerful princelings, corrupt priests, herdsmen and husbandmen besides the select few addressed as initiates.

> "Therefore have I come to you all
> as the enlightened Guide
> appointed by Ahura Mazda
> to judge between these two opposing parties.
> Let us live in harmony with Truth and Justice." (Ys.31.2)

Further, he proclaims himself a Zaotar (Ys.33.6), an officiating priest at a religious ceremony, learned in composing intricate, mantric verses full of meaning.

Even more important, he claims to be a Manthran, a preacher of the Sacred Word, the Manthra, which is "the greatest of all truths" (Ys.28.5; 32.13; 50.5). Hence, Ahura Mazda's dramatic command: "Go, instruct man in the Truth, and reveal teachings hitherto unheard of . . . (Ys.43.12). He also considers himself a seer **éréshi** (Vedic *rishi*) who perceives "what will or will not be" (Ys.31.5).[18]

It is the initiate who receives "the best of doctrines which Ahura, the Giver of Good, teaches through Truth. You, the Benevolent One, reveal the most profound teachings which are Your very own: these which exist in the Wisdom of the Good Mind, O Mazda" (Ys.48.3).

What is more, Zarathushtra considers himself a "friend and ally" of Ahura Mazda, His *Hamkar*, co-worker, (Ys.34.14), appointed by Him to lead all mankind towards the Frashokéréti.

As a preacher, his first doctrine is that there is only One Supreme Being, Ahura Mazda, the embodiment of Life and Wisdom, all-powerful, Benevolent, who governs Man and the Universe through His Powers. This was shocking and utterly unacceptable to his audience who indulged in bloody sacrifices to please those deities they believed gave them plenty and prosperity, and propitiate certain others who inflicted drought, disease and death.

According to the Zoroastrians, Man was given the choice to do good to others or indulge in cruel sacrifices to appease angry deities who inflict death and disease on all creatures as well as plants.

Thus, society was split into two opposing groups: the **Mazda-Yasnas** or Worshippers of Mazda-Ahura and the **Daeva-Yasnas**, Worshippers of the Daevas, false gods. In Hinduism, Daeva means Shining One. In Zoroastrian doctrine, Amesha Spenta implies Immortal Shining Ones. Zarathushtra condemned the Daevas as False Gods. In retaliation, the Hindus demonised the Asuras (Ahuras) once worshipped as the high gods of Truth and Justice. Both the Mazda-Yasnas and the Daeva-Yasnas indulged in bloody sacrifices, specially of the Cow.

Zarathushtra was against the wholesale slaughter of cattle, the most precious worldly possession of the community. He was against Black Magic and drunkenness. Disgusting practices were indulged in during his time. For example, a group of stalwart young men, well armed with heavy clubs, javelins and spears would enter the lair of a wolf on a moonless night, slit its throat and drink its warm blood in the mistaken belief that the strength of the wolf would thereupon enter into their human blood.

The Prophet is in despair in his struggle to eliminate this Savagery and Evil:

> "How, shall I expel untruth from amongst us?"
> "Those who are full of disobedience
>   neither shine in the pursuit of Truth
>   nor delight in the teachings of the Good Mind."   (Ys.44.13)

Again he cries out:

> "Where does comfort replace sorrow?
>   Where does mercy prevail?
>   Where can Truth be attained?
>   Where is your compassionate Devotion?
>   Where is Your Sovereignty, O Mazda,
>   And where your Supreme Mind?"   (Ys.51.4)

All these he asks for so that "law-abiding individuals and their enlightened Guide, the Ratu, through their penetrating insight, control the two rewards (for good and evil)" (Ys.51.5).

Zarathushtra is unique among the founders of the great world religions in that he insists on everyone exercising his freedom of choice, "man by man, each one for his own self" (Ys.30.2) This, of course, not only forces every individual to think for himself/herself, but also to shoulder the responsibility of the results of the action taken. The generality of mankind would rather not take such responsibility. They are only too willing to pass this on to Church and State. To think clearly for oneself is always an arduous task, but immensely rewarding. It gives every individual a sense of total freedom. But the responsibility engendered by the action which follows can become a heavy burden.

Zarathushtra, however, assures us that Ahura Mazda does not abandon men and women in their distress but sends them His Powers to help them make the right choice. He has not only granted every man inner faculties to guide his choice, such as, Daena, conscience, Khratu, intelligence Chisti, insight, Sraosha, the faculty of "hearkening" to the voice of Ahura Mazda, but also placed His Powers within man for that purpose. Moreover, He invites Man to be His Hamkar, co-worker, so that, hand in hand, both may strive to bring about the Frashokéréti. This fellow feeling with Ahura Mazda gives every Zoroastrian an optimistic buoyancy which accompanies him throughout his life. Nothing can go wrong if we place one hand in the hand of Ahura Mazda, and the other in the hand of Asha, Truth, in our daily life, for Ahura Mazda and Truth "are one."

Moreover, Zarathushtra insists that thought, word and deed must be combined into a single unity. The Good Thought, must be expressed in Good Words, and both translated into Good Deeds.

Hence the Motto of the Religion: **Humata, Hukhta, Huvarashta**. The good thought, conceived in the mind, must be spoken so that others may hear it, and then embodied in action so that others may benefit. In the happiness of those around him, man finds his own happiness. So every Zoroastrian is urged to perform as many good deeds as he can throughout his earthly life. There is no other Salvation for him except in the good deeds he performs on earth.

These good deeds must extend not only to one's fellow men, but also to plants and animals. Hence the expression, "the sacred Waters and Plants." So the true Zoroastrian keeps the waters clean and flowing, plants fresh and green, and develops the mineral kingdom and other resources in Nature for the benefit of man. Animals must also be cared for and treated with love.

Moreover, Zarathushtra firmly believes that *getig*, the physical world and *menog*, the mental world, are *one* world, and both are sacred and to be enjoyed. Our bodies must be kept clean and in perfect health to give us the utmost enjoyment. Food is sacred and to be relished, but not to the extent of gluttony so that what is eaten is disgorged. Sex is sacred and meant to be a thrilling experience, but not to be desecrated. Marriage is sacred and designed for the fulfilment of both husband and wife. In the last Gatha which celebrates the marriage of Zarathushtra's youngest daughter, Pouruchista, we read:

> "I address words of advice to the brides, and to you,
>   O bridegrooms,
>   so listen carefully to these teachings.
>   Being well versed in religious doctrines,
>   learn to value the life of the Good Mind.
>   May each of you strive with the other to attain Truth.
>   Indeed, this will be to him or her
>   a blessed existence."   (Ys.53.5)

> In this way, O men and women,
>   you will unite with Truth . . .   (Ys.53.6)

Further, he declares that "silent meditation is best for man". In the extant Gathas there is no mention of techniques of meditation, but at least we are made aware of the importance of developing both body and mind for our fulfilment in life.

Zarathushtra is also emphatic in condemning anger and cruelty:

"Down with Wrath!
Crush cruelty,
you who would maintain through Truth,
the widespread penetration of the Good Mind
in whose company walks the just man.
Such dwell in Your House of Song, O Ahura." (Ys.48.7)

Friendship is considered sacred, and not to be betrayed. The Prophet yearns for Ahura Mazda to treat him as His earthly friend and teach him Wisdom (Ys.44.1). He is Ahura Mazda's "friend and ally" (Ys.31.22) apart from worshipping Him in songs of praise.

Finally, Zarathushtra's idea of the Frashokéréti is unique as it links up man's individual choice with the Renewal of Existence. There can be no mass conversion of the wicked to turn them into the good. Each person must *choose* Truth and the Good Mind individually, and then live by them. When all mankind have fulfilled their destiny by choosing the right, then the Frashokéréti will become a reality. This will be a long, drawn out process.

Therefore, the last word on the Gathas will never be said. To each generation these texts will reveal an aspect of their truth relevant to that generation's specific problems. But the fulfilment of life will always remain the same: a wondrous Renewal of Existence.

Notes

1 R. Grishman, *Iran,* Penguin (Pelican Special, 1954), p. 219.

2 See *The Asian Age* (Delhi ed.) 12th Nov. 1997, p. 4 and *Diary,* India International Centre, Delhi, Vol.XI, No.6, Nov.-Dec. 1997, p. 6. Also Paul G. Bahn, *The Cambridge Illustrated History of Prehistoric Art* Cambridge: 1998 pp. 71

3 See *Dinkart,* Bk. VII. Chap. 2, SBE, Vol. 47, pp. 17-35; *Selections from Zadspram,* SBE, ibid, pp. 133-170. *Zarathust-nama,* compiled by Zarthusht-i-Bahram-i-Pazdu. See Marijan Mole, *Culte, Mythe et Cosmologie dans I' Iran ancien,* Presses Universitaires de France, Paris, 1963, pp. 276-347.

4 H.K.Mirza, "Ancient Iranian Systems of Writing,." *Journal of the K.R. Cama Oriental Institute,* Vol. 47, Bombay, 1979, p. 23

5 Harvey p. Alper, *Mantra* Albany NY, 1987 pp. 21-37

6 Stanley Isler, *The Gathas of Zarathusthra,* Acta Iranica, 3rd Series, Vol. I Leiden, p. 25, n.2.

7 Helmut Humbach, *Gathas,* II, pp. 177, 220.

8 Arda Viraf was a learned, much travelled and very respected priest in Sasanian times. He was also very saintly, so he was chosen by his peers to explore Heaven and Hell and the after life, return to earth and describe what he saw. He was given narcotics and put into a trance, watched day and night by a relay of priests till he woke. His adventures are embodied in the *Arda Viraf Nama.* This text exists in both the original Pahlavi and in various Gujarati versions, all in manuscript form. For a critical survey, see Vahman (Fereydun), *Arda Wiraz Namag* the Iranian "divina commedia," London, Curzon Press, 1986 (Scandinavian Institute of Asian Studies, Monograph Series, No.53). This study contains the original Pahlavi Text (facsimile), with translation, commentary, glossary and index. A copy is housed in the Library of the Indira Gandhi National Centre for the Arts, New Delhi.

9 Barsom is derived from the Avestan *Barsam,* meaning "to grow" Some Pahlavi Texts assert that the twigs of the pomegranate may be used. Others mention the Chini tree. As neither of these is found on the West coast of India where the Iranian Zoroastrian refugees settled, the priests substituted, and still use thin, metallic wires, copper, brass or silver, nine inches long, for the Barsom twigs. According to the religious ritual to be performed, these metallic wires are tied with the fronds of the Palm Tree, in

bundles of three, five, seven, nine or more. The bundles are placed on the Mahrui, a crescent-shaped metal stand, symbolising the Moon. The Barsom represents the vegetable kingdom while the Moon was believed to influence the growth of plants, specially the Haoma (Vedic *Soma*), whose twigs filled with sap on full moon nights. See J.J. Modi, *The Religious Ceremonies and Customs of the Parsees,* Bombay, 1921, reprint 1986, pp. 261-268; 253

10 See n. 9

11 See J.J. Modi, *Religious Ceremonies* pp. 218-226.

12 See *Aerpatastan and Nirangistan,* tr.Sohrab Jamshedjee Bulsara, Bombay, 1921 BK, III chap. VII, Appendix A, p. 436.

13 J Duchesne-Guillemin, "Symbole et Mythe dans l'Iran ancient," *Orientalia Romana* Essays and Lectures, No.5, Iranian Studies, Roma, 1983, pp. 1-9.

14 The Chistiya Order among the Sufis developed this concept still further.

15 The reference is to the juice of the Haoma Plant which drunk in excess caused intoxication.

16 M.N. Dhalla, *Zoroastrian Theology,* New York, 1914, pp. 38, 39.

17 See J. Darmesteter, *Zend Avesta* Vol.I, p. 128, n.5.

18 I owe this reference to Farrokh Jal Vajifdar.

The Legend of Gaush Urva
The Creation Story

Ahura Mazda, the embodiment of Life and Wisdom, uncreated and eternal, lives in Everlasting Light.

He wished to manifest Himself, so He brought forth six Divine Powers: Vohu Mana, The Good Mind; Asha, Cosmic Order, Truth, Justice; Khashathra, Sovereignty, Kingdom, Power; Armaiti, Love, Devotion, Piety, Zeal; Haurvatat; Perfection, and, Ameretat, Immortality, Himself being the seventh and Supreme Power including all.

From Vohu Mana, The Good Mind, movement entered the static world of matter. From the essence of the material world, He first created the Sky which is celestial Fire. Secondly He created the Element Water, third the Earth, fourth Plants, fifth Cattle, sixth Man. From the boundless, everlasting Light, He created Fire in manifest form. The first material creation was water, from which arose all things, except the seed of man and cattle, for that seed has the seed of Fire in it.

He then fashioned the "uniquely created Bull" **Gav-i-evdad**, corrupted to Gav-yo-dad/Gayodad, from the Earth on the banks of the river **Daiti** (Oxus) which runs through the middle of the Earth. The Bull was white and shining like the Moon, and his height was about three cubits.

Next He fashioned **Gayomard**, mortal man, from the Earth, on the banks of the river Daiti which is in the middle of the Earth. Gayomard was about four cubits tall, and his width was about three cubits.

Then from the light and freshness of the Sky, He fashioned the seed of man and bulls, for these seeds have their origin in Fire,

not in water. He placed the seeds in the bodies of the Man and the Bull so that there would be abundant progeny for men and cattle.

All at once, from the bowels of the Earth, there burst forth Angra Mainyu, the Hostile Spirit.[1] He poured forth an avalanche of evils on Gayomard, the Man and on Gayodad, the Bull, evils of greed, gluttony, pain, disease, lust and sloth. On the plants he cast a blight and such poison that they withered away in an instant. But even as they were dying, they said: "By the moisture that belongs to Ahura Mazda, He will cause us to grow again."

On Gayomard and Gayodad Angra Mainyu poured more calamities: lechery, want, pain, disease and sloth. Gayomard with his last breath proclaimed: "The Aggressor has come now, but men will arise from my seed and it is best for them to do good works."

But before Angra Mainyu could reach Gayodad, the Bull, Ahura Mazda gave him *bang*[2] to chew. He rubbed some of the leaves on the animal's eyes so that he would suffer less from Angra Mainyu's tortures.

The Bull grew pale and sickened, but his pain was short lived. Straightaway he died, but with his dying breath he uttered these words: "Let the actions and deeds of men work for perfect rule over the animal creation."

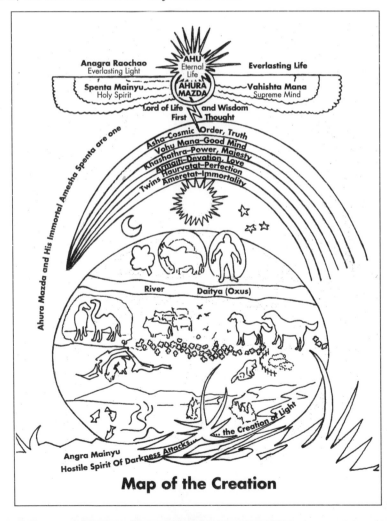

Map of the Creation

Yet all was not lost. From the dead body of the Bull, there rose his living soul, Gaush Urva. She stood before the body, and, in a voice like that of an army of a thousand men crying out loud together, she questioned Ahura Mazda:

"In whose hands have You trusted the care of Your creatures now that ruin has penetrated the Earth, plants withered and the waters troubled? Where is he, the Man (Zarathushtra), whom You had promised: 'I will bring him forth so that he may teach mankind reverence and care for every thing that lives: every leaf and flower, every bird in the air, every fish in the waters, every four-footed animal that roams the earth'?"

Ahura Mazda replied:

"You are ill, O Gaush Urva. You suffer from the sickness which the Evil Spirit has brought upon you. The time has not yet come for me to bring forth the Man who will teach reverence and care for every thing that lives. Be patient."

But Gaush Urva turned away in anger and despair. At one stride she reached the Station of the Stars and in a voice like the war cry of an army of a thousand men she called for help. But the stars darkened and hung their heads in misery. They could not help Gaush Urva.

Forth went Gaush Urva and at one stride reached the Station of the Moon. Crying out with the voice of a thousand men, she demanded help. But the Moon covered her face with clouds and shed secret tears. She could not help Gaush Urva.

Forth went Gaush Urva, and with one stride reached the Station of the Sun. There the **Fravashi**[3] of Zarathushtra appeared before her. She gazed in wonder at the angelic form. From the golden depths of the Sun came the voice of Ahura Mazda: "For the sake of the world I will produce him who will teach reverence and care for every thing that lives."

Then was Gaush Urva content. She said to herself: "I will go down to the Earth and nourish the creatures." She collected the seed of the Man from the Sun, and the seed of the Bull from the Moon and returned to the Earth. There she called upon **Mino Raam**, the spirit of abounding peace, and together they distributed the seed of the Man and the seed of the Bull throughout the Earth.

The waters began to flow. They sparkled in the springs, gleamed in the winding rivers and flowed in fullness to the sea. The land burst into leaf, flower and fruit. Animals in droves roamed the forests and the pasture lands. Birds of many coloured plumage flew in the sky. Silver scaled fish leapt and danced in the rivers and lakes. Gaush Urva smiled. A great happiness stole into her heart as she gazed upon her children.

But Angra Mainyu nursed revenge. Again he attacked the Earth and all her creatures. The waters dried up. Plants withered. Men and animals died by the hundred. Their bleached bones lay scattered on plain and hillside. The parched Earth cracked and was burnt black by the scorching Sun. Desolation stalked the land. Gaush Urva sat in the midst of this desolation and waited for the Man, Zarathushtra, who would teach reverence and care for every thing that lives.[4]

Notes

1 Cf. Mara in Buddhism, Lucifer in Judaism, Satan in Christianity, Iblis in Islam.

2 Bhang, a narcotic plant.

3 The Guardian Spirit in every man and all Creation.

4 The above legend, occasionally elaborated, is based on Pahlavi Texts written in the ninth and tenth centuries. These Texts contain fragments of ancient myths faithfully recorded by the priests. See *Bundahishn*, I, 32, 33, 41, 49, 51; III, 12, 16; IV. 2, 3, 8, 9, 11. *Zadspram*, 11, 13. Cf. *Dinkart*, IX.51. My grateful thanks go to Farrokh Jal Vajifdar for his help with the references.

Gatha Ahunavaiti

The Gatha of Free Choice
The Lament of Gaush Urva: Text
Yasna 29

1   To You, O Divine Powers, Gaush Urva cried out in anguish:
"For whom have You brought me into being?
Who shaped me?
Wrath and Rapine, Aggression and Violence[1] crush me.
No one is my protector
except You, O Lord,
so reveal to me the caring herdsman."

2   Then her creator, Gaush Tasha, questioned Truth:
"Who will be the protective guide
of these herds?
When will you appoint a good and loving herdsman
to nourish them?
Who will foster them with zeal?
Who will be their longed-for Lord
who will overcome the fury
of the wicked?"[2]

3   Truth, who neither wounds nor is hostile, replied:
"I know none here who would guide men in their life.
Indeed, he must be a most powerful and upright man
if I, Truth, answer his cry for help."

4   Mazda is the supreme knower of all actions,
past and present,
performed by men and even by the Daevas.[3]
He is the sole discriminating Lord
of such misguided individuals.
As He wills, so be it.

5   With outstretched hands invoking Ahura
     may my soul and that of the fertile herds reach His Wisdom
     and place before Him these searching questions:
     "Does no harm come to those who live righteously?
     Nor to the herdsman though he dwells
     in the midst of the wicked?"

6   Ahura Mazda, the Omniscient,
     who through His powerful insight
     knows the final outcome, answered:
     "Not a single Lord, Ahu, nor an enlightened Guide (Ratu),
     who walks hand in hand with Truth,
     has yet been found to help Gaush Urva.
     I have, therefore, appointed you, (Zarathushtra)
     as her protector and herdsman.

7   Ahura Mazda is one with Truth.
     As a sacrificial offering
     He lavishes the sweet nourishment of butter and milk
     upon the needy.
     For the enlightened He frames His Decrees."
     (Gaush Urva questioned)
     "O Good Mind, whom have you proclaimed
     as protector over me and my herds before all mankind?"

8   "Here, one man alone has listened to our Decrees.
     He is Spitama Zarathushtra.
     He is eager to proclaim
     the glory of Mazda and His Truth
     so let him be blest with sweetness of speech."

9   Gaush Urva wailed:
     "Now must I submit to an ineffectual leader,
     to the words of a feeble man!
     I long for a powerful ruler.
     When, if ever, will he come who will help me
     with the might of his hands?"

10   (Gaush Urva, reconciled speaks:)
   "O Ahura, grant Zarathushtra and his followers
   eminence and Sovereignty through Truth.
   May they establish a peaceful and happy existence
   through the Good Mind.
   I recognise You, O Mazda,
   as the prime giver of this gift."

11   (Then Zarathushtra arose and said):
   "Where are Truth, Good Mind and the Sovereignty?
   O man, accept the new teaching of enlightenment
   offered by Mazda as a sacramental duty.[4]
   And You, O Ahura, come to our aid
   in return for our praise and worship of You."

Notes

1   Tevishi, (Vedic *tavishi*), violence or brutality, is used again by Zarathushtra in Ys.33.12 as moral courage or ardent desire. For an explanation see Introduction.

2   An indirect allusion to the *mairyas,* (Vedic *maryas*), marauding border tribes who would descend during autumn on the peaceful villagers, slaughter their men folk, carry away their women and children to be used as slaves, and their cattle for food during the hard, cold, winter months in the mountain fastnesses they inhabited (Cf. Ys.53.8 and 9). As Mary Boyce points out: "changing social conditions appear to have led Zoroaster to challenge and to change an old Indo-Iranian concept namely that of Indra as the patron god of the young men *(maryas)* of the tribe, so that from a mighty and kind helper he became a potent and wicked stirrer up of strife" (Boyce, *Zoroastrianism, Its Antiquity and Constant Vigour*, Mazda Publishers, Costa Mesa, California and New York, 1992, p. 61, n.24. See also pp.39, 56, 59).

3   Daeva means "shining one" and is applied to Hindu deities in the Vedas, and also in common parlance to this day. Zarathushtra uses the word to signify False Gods, and the Worshippers of False Gods, the *Daeva-yasni.*

4   See Maga in Introduction.

Zarathushtra at Prayer
Yasna 28
Commentary

Zarathushtra is very conscious of his mission on earth which is to teach mankind reverence and care for every thing that lives. He has just received the blessings of Gaush Urva, who represents the sufferings of all Creation.

For the first time we are introduced to Zoroastrian doctrine to understand which we need to know something about the society in which Zarathushtra lived. There were the shepherd and herdsmen on the one hand, and the learned Kavis, together with the Karapans, on the other. All believed in many gods, some benevolent, others evil. Both powers had to be placated with bloody sacrifices of the cow or ox.

Against this background, Zarathushtra boldly preached of one Supreme Being, Ahura Mazda, Lord of Life and Wisdom who is united with Asha, Truth and Cosmic Order. Ahura Mazda rules the universe through His benevolent Powers, the Amesha Spenta, Immortal Shining Ones. These are: Asha, Truth and Cosmic Order; Vohu Mana, the Good Mind, representing Ahura Mazda's goodness towards the whole of Creation; Khashathra, Sovereignty, Power, which destroys evil; and Armaiti, Love and Devotion. These four Powers are latent in every man and accompany him throughout his earthly life. They will lead him to the twin goals of Haurvatat, Perfection, and Amérétat, Immortality. The Divine Powers are not cold abstractions, but living entities with whom Zarathushtra converses as with a friend: "Truth, when shall I see you? And you, O Good Mind, ripe in wisdom?" (Ys.28.5)

Zarathushtra is unique in insisting that both the physical body and the mind must be linked. He therefore dedicates his body and mind to Asha, the Truth, through whom Ahura Mazda leads man to the light of knowledge, and self-awareness.

We are now introduced to a basic Gathic concept, the Manthra, the Sacred Word of Power, embodied in the Holy Scriptures. Through the Manthra "men with the poisonous tongues of vipers turn from violence to true faith" (Ys.28.5)

Another basic concept, Sava, salvation, is introduced as the birthright of every man provided he turns to Ahura Mazda for that gift (Ys.28.9).

Zarathushtra insists that both body and mind are sacred. Both must work in unison with the Divine Powers through the Manthra embedded in the Scriptures. Salvation is assured to all provided we turn to Ahura Mazda and His Sovereignty for that gift. The chapter ends with Zarathushtra dedicating himself anew to Ahura Mazda and His Powers. They will help him to proclaim what spiritual life on earth should be (Ys.28.11).

Zarathushtra at Prayer: Text
Yasna 28

1   With hands outstretched in reverence, O Mazda,
I pray for the abiding support of Your ever-expanding
Spirit of Benediction.
All my actions I dedicate to Truth.
May the Wisdom of the Good Mind guide me.
So may I gladden Gaush Urva.[1]

2   O Ahura Mazda, may I reach You,
in fullness of knowledge that comes from the Good Mind.
Let the dual life of my body and mind
receive the blessings of Your Truth
through which You lead all mankind into the Light.

3   I shall offer, as was never done before,
songs of praise to you, O Good Mind,
and to you, O Truth, and to You O Mazda Ahura.
For it is You who make Devotion bloom,
and You who strengthen Your immeasurable Sovereignty.
So descend, O Powers.
Hear my prayer. Uphold me.

4   I will sing Your praise
uniting myself to the Good Mind. Bless this work
begun in Your name, O Mazda Ahura. As long as I have
the will and the strength
so long will I preach the search for Truth.

5   Truth, when shall I see you?
And you, O Good Mind, ripe in wisdom?
You know the path which leads
to the most exalted Ahura, through willing obedience
to Mazda.
May we reveal that greatest of all truths,

the Sacred Word, which makes
even men with the poisonous tongue of vipers
turn from violence to true faith.

6   Come, Spirit of Eternal life,[2]
come, O Ahura, with the Good Mind and bless us
with Your Truth's everlasting gifts.
Your hallowed words, O Mazda, bring strong support
to Zarathushtra and to us, his followers.
Give us the means to vanquish
the hatred of our enemies.

7   Grant, O Truth, that blessing
which is the reward of the Good Mind.
O holy Devotion, strengthen Vishtaspa[3] and me.
And You, O Mazda,
grant us power to spread abroad
Your Sacred Word.

8   Most exalted are You, O Ahura,
and one with Supreme Truth.
Lovingly I entreat You
to grant the manly Frashaoshtra
and me and my followers
the possession of the Good Mind for ever.

9   O Ahura Mazda,
never may we provoke You by these entreaties
neither You, nor Truth, nor Your Supreme Mind.
We have striven earnestly
to sing Your praise
calling upon You and Your Sovereignty
for our salvation.

10   O Ahura Mazda,
bless those who cherish the Good Mind
and seek Righteousness.

I know that hymns chanted to You from the heart
are always heard.

11 O Ahura Mazda,
I will uphold Your Truth and Your Good Mind for ever.
With Your very own mouth and tongue
speak the inspired word. Teach me to proclaim
how the foremost existence (spiritual life on this earth)
will be.

Notes

1 Gaush Urva here represents not only the Soul of Cattle, but also the Drighu, the poor and the downtrodden, crying out for justice. See Introduction.

2 D.J. Irani's fine phrase.

3 Vishtaspa was the kavi or princeling of Bactria (Afghanisatan). His family and the entire court were converted to Zarathushtra's teachings. Two senior ministers at Vishtaspa's Court were Jamaspa and Frashaoshtra, brothers. According to Zoroastrian tradition, Pouruchista, Zarathushtra's youngest daughter, married Jamaspa. (See S.B.E. Vols.XXIII, pp. 204-205, 306; XXXVI, pp. 219, 236, 406, 413).

The Origin of Evil
Yasna 30
Commentary

This is a very important *Ha*, or chapter, in the Gathas for it presents Zarathushtra's explanation of the origin of evil. He makes use of an ancient myth, that of the Twin Mainyu or Mentalities. These are the dual aspects of the human mind: the desire to do good, and the desire to do evil. Man must choose between them.

According to the legend, these Twin Mentalities revealed themselves "in vision" as "the better and the bad" in thought, word and deed. Then they came together and established **gaya** or mortal life which vanishes at the time of physical death, and **ajyaiti**, non-life. Gaya must be distinguished from Ahu, eternal life which cannot be destroyed. Every individual has to choose between Good and Evil. The wise chose correctly but the unwise did not.

Now Angra Mainyu, the Hostile or Evil Spirit, "elected" to perform the worst deeds. But the Most Bountiful Spirit who dwells in imperishable Light, chose Truth. And so did those who rejoiced Ahura Mazda with their deeds (Ys.30.5)

The Daevas, signifying false gods and their worshippers, did not distinguish wisely between these two Mentalities. Confusion came upon them as they debated and so they chose the Worst Mind, the most darkened mind (*achista mana*). As a result, they fell headlong into Wrath and so poisoned the life of plant, animal and man. (Ys.30.6)

The just are however not abandoned . Ahura Mazda comes to their help through the Good Mind and Truth, while His "daughter" Armaiti, (Love and Devotion) gives man's subtle body the enduring breath of life (Ys.30.7)

Mankind cannot escape the consequences of evil actions.

Retribution follows. But the Good Mind and Truth ensure the Sovereignty of Ahura to those who "deliver the Lie into the hands of Truth" (Ys.30.8).

He who cherishes all life, plant, animal and man, will renew the Earth. Such individuals will receive "illumined insight" when their perceptions grown dim, for Mazda will come to them with all the Lords of Life for their enlightenment (Ys.30.9).

The prosperity of the wicked will be destroyed. But the Follower of Truth will share in the promised reward and dwell with the Good Mind, Truth and Wisdom (Ys.30.10).

This chapter concludes with a prophecy. Men's actions will lead to happiness or misery, both controlled by Divine Decrees. The wicked will suffer, while the just will attain salvation (Sava). Thereafter, eternal bliss shall prevail everywhere.

The Origin of Evil: Text
Yasna 30

1   I will now declare to earnest listeners, and even to the
    initiate,
    concerning the adoration and praise due to Ahura
    through the Good Mind. And I will reach out to those
    who, by means of wisdom,
    gaze upon the light of Truth
    and so attain perfect bliss.

2   Listen to the noblest teachings
    with an attentive ear.
    With your penetrating mind[1] discriminate
    between these twin mentalities,
    man by man, each one for his own self.
    Awake, to proclaim this Truth
    before the Final Judgement overtakes you.

3   Now in the beginning
    these two mentalities, the twins, revealed themselves
    in vision as the better and the bad
    in thought, word and deed. The wise and the
    generous chose correctly between these two, but the
    unwise
    and the mean did not.

4   And so
    when these two mentalities first came together,
    they established life (*gaya*) and non-life (*ajyaiti*).
    The worst life will be
    for the Followers of the Lie,
    but the Supreme Mind of Ahura Mazda
    will illumine the Followers of Truth.

5   From these two mentalities
the Evil One elected to perform the worst deeds.
But the Most Bountiful Spirit
who dwells in imperishable Light
chose Truth.
And so did those who rejoiced Ahura Mazda
by their devoted actions.

6   The Daevas (and their worshippers)
did not discriminate wisely
between these two. Confusion came upon them
as they debated,
and so they chose the Worst Mind.
Straightaway, they fell headlong into Wrath.
The life of man sickened.

7   Then the Sovereignty of Ahura came to the just man
through the Good Mind and Truth.
Compassionate Devotion gave his subtle body
the sustaining breath of life. At the time of the
Reckoning,[2]
Ahura Mazda will be there as the First One (to help
man).

8   When retribution overtakes these sinners,
O Mazda, then Your Truth
and the Good Mind will ensure the Sovereignty
to those who deliver the Lie
into the hands of Truth.

9   Hence,
may we be those who renew this earthly life.
Then Mazda and the Lords[3] will come with Truth
bringing their support of illumined insight
where perception remains uncertain.

10   Then indeed will the prosperity of the wicked be
destroyed.
Then too,

the widely acclaimed Followers of Truth
will share in the promised reward
and dwell with the Good Mind, Truth and Wisdom.

11   So understand, O mortal men, the Decrees
which Mazda has established regarding happiness and
misery.
There will be
a long period of suffering for the wicked,
and salvation for the just,
but thereafter
eternal bliss shall prevail everywhere.

Notes

1   The phrase, *sucha manangha*, translated as penetrating mind, clear mind, does not bring out the full meaning. Humbach draws attention to Rig-Veda, 3-4-1, where "sucha . . . sucha" is used for Agni (Fire), in the sense of "ray" or "radiance", so he translates the Gathic phrase "through the radiance of your thought" (See H. Humbach, Elfenbein & Skjaerve, *The Gathas of Zarathushtra*, 2nd ed. 2 Vols. Heidelberg, 1991, Vol.II, p. 47. Cf. Ys.46.7 where Atar, Fire, is linked with Manangha, Mind).

2.   The Reckoning refers to the final purification of mankind when the just and the unjust will both have to pass through red-hot molten metal. To the just, it will seem like "warm milk" but not so to the wicked.

3   Ahura in the plural.

The Choice
Yasna 31
Commentary

This chapter reveals Zarathushtra's understanding of the difficulties faced by human beings in making a just choice between the Decrees of Mazda and the deceitful Decrees of the Worshippers of Falsehood. Zarathushtra proclaims himself a Ratu, the enlightened Guide, appointed by Ahura Mazda to judge between the two opposing parties (Ys.31.1 and 2).

The next four verses explain how Ahura Mazda's "hidden Fire and Truth" help each individual to make a true choice. In Ys.31.5 Zarathushtra proclaims himself as a visionary, a seer, who has insight into the future, This is the only instance in the entire Avesta where **éréshi**, Vedic *Rishi*, is used. (Ys.31.3–6).

Zarathushtra's views on the Creation are now stated. The entire Cosmos, Nature, Man, Animal, Vegetable and Mineral Kingdoms, are the result of Ahura Mazda's First Thought which "blazed into myriads of sparks of light." Thus the Fravashis were born, Guardian Spirits guiding and protecting every atom of existence. (Ys.31–7).

In the next verse Zarathushtra holds Ahura Mazda "in his mind's eye" and so realises that He is the "First and the Last for all Eternity as the Father of the Good Mind, the true Creator of Truth and Lord over the actions of life." (Ys.31.8).

The emphasis on choice is again stressed and extended even to the Cow who chooses her herdsman with care, "a Master in Righteousness who furthers the work of the Good Mind." (Ys.31.10). In this context the Cow seems to represent the community as well, for only members of the community can choose a Master in Righteousness. It is well known that among the Essenes, a mystical Jewish sect who flourished in the early

Christian centuries, there were Zoroastrian practices such as bathing before meals, eating in silence (holding the baj), facing the East when praying, etc. There was also a "Master in Righteousness" whose function it was to see that all members observed ritual purity, adhered to strict moral principles, and brought all differences to the Master of Righteousness to solve. (See A. Dupont Somer, *Les Ecrits Esséniennes*, Payot, Paris, 1980, pp. 136ff).

The Prophet explains how Ahura Mazda has equipped every individual from birth with certain faculties which help in making the right choice (Ys.31.11-13).

At this point a series of questions to Ahura Mazda are raised about the consequences of one's choice (Ys.31.14-17).

Zarathushtra warns his listeners not to heed the Worshippers of Falsehood for they will "deliver the home, the town, the province and the country to strife and destruction" (Ys.31.18).

The concluding verses depict the condition of the Followers of Truth **(Ashavans)** as dwelling in heavenly Light, while the Followers of the Lie **(Dregvants)** will suffer "a long life of darkness, foul food and woeful wailings" in **Drujo-Demana**, the House of the Lie, after death (Ys.31.19-20).

The Choice: Text
Yasna 31

1   We keep in mind these Decrees of Yours, O Ahura,
words unheard so far –.
We proclaim them
to those who destroy the Truth-seekers
by deceitful means.
These sacred Decrees are best
for those who trust in Mazda.

2   The better path can neither be seen nor chosen
because of these deceitful Decrees (of the
Worshippers of Falsehood).
Therefore have I come to you all
as the chosen Guide
appointed by Ahura Mazda
to judge between these two opposing parties.
Let us live in harmony with Truth and Justice.

3   O Ahura, You offer that harmony
to each of these two contenders
by means of Your hidden Fire and Truth
in keeping with Your Decrees.
O Mazda,
with Your very own mouth and tongue
proclaim this to us
for our enlightenment.
Thus I will convince all the living (regarding true faith).

4   I will invoke You, O Mazda,
and You O Ahuras,[1]
as also Justice and its rewards,
and holy Devotion. Then I will seek Your Supreme Mind
through whose Sovereignty
we may conquer the Lie.

5   Speak, O Mazda Ahura,
on what I should perceive as the nobler guidance
created for me by Truth
for my understanding
in keeping with the Good Mind.
For I am the éréshi (rishi),
endowed with visionary insight
into what will or will not be.[2]

6   The best shall befall the initiate
who spreads abroad My true and Sacred Word
relating to Perfection, Immortality and Truth.
Thus the might of Mazda will grow
within him through the Good Mind.

7   Ahura Mazda's First Thought
blazed into myriads of sparks of light
and filled the entire heavens.[3]
He Himself, in His Wisdom,
is the Creator of Truth which
upholds His Supreme Mind.
O Ahura Mazda,
You who are eternally the same,
further these Powers through Your Truth.

8   When I held You in my mind's eye
then I realised You, O Mazda,
as the First and the Last for all Eternity,
as the Father of the Good Mind,
the true Creator of Truth,
and Lord over the actions of life.

9   O Ahura Mazda,
since to You belongs Devotion,
to You the Creator of Cattle,
and to You the dynamism of the Spirit,
therefore you gave her (the Cow),
the choice of a way,
either to stay with the caring herdsman

or with him who never was one.

10   So from these two she chose for herself
a Master in Righteousness
who furthers
the work of the Good Mind.
O Mazda,
the sly, self-deceiving non-herdsman
cannot share in Your Good Message
despite longing for it.

11   O Mazda, from the beginning
You fashioned for us
physical bodies, an awakened conscience and a
directive intelligence
through Your own Mind.
You infused life breath
into mortal forms.
You granted us
capacities to act and true teachings to guide us
so that we could choose to be with You or against You.

12   Since then,
each lifts up his voice to proclaim his faith,
both the liar and the truth-speaker,
whether learned or unlearned,
according to his own heart and mind.
But compassionate Devotion stands by
to deliberate with the spirit
of whoever is perplexed by doubt.

13   Whether we deliberate openly or secretly, O Mazda,
or whether one endures
severe punishment for a trifling fault,
You observe all
with a penetrating Eye through Your Truth.

14 These I ask You, O Ahura:
   What takes place and what is yet to be?
   What rewards are gained by the Truth-seekers?
   And what of the retribution earned by the
   Worshippers of Falsehood?
   In what manner are these considered at the Final
   Judgement?

15 These I ask, O Ahura:
   What will he suffer who advances
   the power of the Worshipper of Falsehood, the
   Evil-doer?
   What will be the punishment of him
   who finds no work
   other than harming the cattle and men[4]
   of the non-deceiving herdsman?

16 This I ask:
   Who is the wise counsellor
   who seeks to further Your Sovereignty
   in the home, the province and the country
   striving to spread Righteousness?
   By such action
   will he become one like You, O Ahura Mazda?

17 Which of the two paths
   does the Truth-seeker and the Worshipper of
   Falsehood
   choose as the better one?
   Let the initiated address the initiate,
   but no longer let the uninitiated lead men astray.
   O Mazda Ahura,
   be the Revealer of the Good Mind for our sake.

18 Let no man listen
   to the unholy incantations of the Worshipper of
   Falsehood
   for he will deliver
   the home, the town, the province and the country

to strife and destruction.
So cut him down with your weapon.

19 O Ahura,
may they listen attentively to the initiate
who contemplates Truth.
He is the Healer of Life
who empowers the true doctrine by his speech.
O Mazda, by means of Your Fire blazing within You
allot their destinies to the two contenders.

20 Whoever clings to the Followers of Truth,
his dwelling shall be the Light.
But for you,
O Worshippers of Falsehood,
a long life of darkness, foul food and woeful wailings –
to such an existence
will your evil conscience
lead you through your own deeds.

21 But to him who is His friend
in thought and act
Ahura Mazda will grant
Perfection and Immortality,
and out of His Abundance Truth,
His Sovereignty and the firm support
of the Good Mind.

22 These things are clear to the wise man
as also to him who acquires the full realisation
of the Good Mind.
Such a person
upholds Truth and Sovereignty
through his word and deed.
He will be
Your most helpful friend and ally, O Ahura Mazda.

Notes

1   Ahura in the plural signifying
    Lords of Life. cf. Y.30.9. n.4.

2   I owe this insight to Farrokh Jal
    Vajifdar cf. Humbach *Gathas*
    1959 ed. Index – éréshi, Indic
    rishi

3   This sentence may seem a
    contradiction to the traditional
    belief that Ahura Mazda lives in
    Undying Light (Anagra
    Raocha-o). Here Zarathushtra
    seems to be saying that the
    ever-present, eternal light
    surrounding Ahura Mazda was
    "personalised" into individual

sparks later named Fravashis.
Every atom of existence has its
own particular Fravashi which
remains pure and incorruptible.
The word, Fravashi, is not
mentioned in the Gathas.

4   The above is a literal translation
    of the common term, *pashu-vira*,
    cattle and men. The Parsi
    phrase, still current, is
    gai-goshpand, the cow and
    cattle. The Hindu phrase is
    gai-dhor, the cow and (her)
    herds.

Zarathushtra's Dedication: I
Yasna 32
Commentary

In this chapter Zarathushtra describes the struggle for supremacy between the Ashavans, Followers of Truth, and the Dregvants, Followers of the Lie. The Daevas, False Gods (the Shining Ones in Hindu thought but demonised by Zarathushtra) also join in this struggle for power. Ironically, they too pray to Ahura Mazda for bliss (Ys.32.1). In post-Vedic literature, the Hindus, in retaliation, demonised the Asuras/Ahuras, originally high gods of Truth and Justice.

Zarathushtra explains how the Daevas and their followers are misled by the Spirit of Falsehood who promises sovereignty to the Followers of the Lie through evil thought, evil word and evil deed (Ys.32.5).

The Prophet next alludes to Yima (Vedic *Yama*), the Jamshid of the *Shah-Nameh,* and his crime of the Bull Sacrifice. He roundly denounces him saying that he will have to answer for his actions at the Last Judgement (Ys.32.8). Zarathushtra also condemns the false teacher who misleads by his evil teachings (Ys.32.9). He warns the Kavis and the Karapans (princes and corrupt priests) that they will view their "ill-gotten wealth" in the dwelling of the Worst Mind at the time of death and moan their loss (Ys.32.13).

Finally, he asserts that the teaching of the devout is the best for the intelligent man. The last sentence is a touching appeal to Ahura Mazda. who holds the mastery over those who threaten the Prophet with destruction. Zarathushtra requests that he be given the same divine power to repulse the wicked from harming any of his followers who long for Ahura Mazda. (Ys.32.16)

Zarathushtra's Dedication: I Text
Yasna 32

1   And so the family, the community and the clan
    pray to Him, Ahura Mazda.
    Even the Daevas pray to Him for bliss.
    May we be Your messengers
    repelling those hostile to You, O Ahura.

2   Then Ahura Mazda,
    uniting with His Good Mind,
    and through His Sovereignty, replied:
    In close companionship with the Sun of Truth[1]
    we have chosen for you, the Truth-seekers,
    the good and loving Devotion.
    'May she be ours', they cried.

3   O Daevas, you are all
    the offspring of the Evil Mind.
    Whoever praises you
    is born of the Lie,
    full of arrogance.
    You are dishonoured for ever
    in the seven regions of the earth[2]
    because of your wicked acts.

4   Thus you corrupted these men
    so that, enacting the worst,
    they are called Beloved of the Daevas.
    They reject
    the Will of Ahura and His Truth
    having withdrawn from the Good Mind.

5   In this way,
    you cheated mankind of the good life and Immortality.
    The Spirit of Falsehood
    also misled you, O Daevas,

through evil thought, evil word and evil deed
when he promised sovereignty
to the Followers of the Lie.

6   The inveterate sinner
tries hard to win renown.
But You, O Ahura, who care for the living,
know his true worth through the Good Mind.
Without a shadow of doubt,
Your Sovereignty and Truth
will spread Your Doctrine among all men.

7   Let the initiate commit
none of these sins to win renown.
On the contrary,
he must strive for the prize
gained by submitting to the fiery ordeal of molten
metal.[3]
O Ahura Mazda, You know best
the final end of such sinners.

8   Among those guilty of such sins,
Yima,[4] son of Vivanghvant,[5]
is notorious.
He permitted the Bull Sacrifice
to gratify the desire of his people (to become
immortal by eating the consecrated flesh of the slain
Bull).
 I separate myself from such sinners
knowing what will come to them at
the Final Judgment, O Mazda.

9   The false teacher
destroys the true doctrine,
and through his evil teachings
the purpose of life as well.
He obstructs all who strive for the Good Mind.
So with this cry from my soul
I reach out to You, O Mazda, and to Your Truth.

10 Indeed, such a man
   destroys the true doctrine when he declares it is most
   wicked
   to gaze at the herds and the Sun with both eyes.[6]
   He turns
   the wise into the deceitful,
   desolates pastures, and threatens
   the righteous with weapons.

11 Without a moment's hesitation,
   the Worshippers of Falsehood wreck life.
   They conspire mightily together
   depriving men and women of their rightful, spiritual
   inheritance.
   O Mazda, they corrupt the Truth-seekers
   who cling to Your Supreme Mind.

12 By such deceitful teaching they divert men
   from the best course of action.
   Mazda has foretold
   the evil they will suffer
   when they destroy the life of the cow
   with exultant shrieks.
   The Worshippers of Falsehood prefer
   the power of the illicitly wealthy[7] Karapans[8]
   instead of the Truth.

13 The destroyers of this life
   will view their ill-gotten wealth
   in the dwelling of the Worst Mind
   to which their evil rule has led them.
   Yet they will continue to cry out
   for the message of Your Manthra-reciter, Zarathushtra.
   Their own deeds
   will prevent them from seeing the Truth.

14 Even these Kavis[9]
   with their unlawful wealth
   have directed their will and their efforts to destroy him

(Zarathushtra),
by aiding the Worshippers of Falsehood.
They have said:
"Let the Cow be killed for the one who kindles the 'Death-
dispeller.'"[10]

15 Thus the clans of the Karapans and the Kavis
are brought to ruin
together with those whom they mislead.
They will never be
among the ones who rule life at will
in the realms of the Good Mind.

16 The teaching of the devout
is indeed best for the intelligent man.
O Ahura Mazda,
You who hold the mastery
over those who threaten me with destruction,
may I too
repulse the wicked from harming
any of my followers
who long for You.

Notes

1 Zarathushtra associates the Sun not only with Truth, but also with Wisdom as in Ys.50.2. In non-Gathic passages of the *Yasna*, the Sun is described as the "Eye of Ahura Mazda" (Ys.1.11; 3.13; 7.13). In the *Rig Veda*, the Sun is the "Eye of Varuna" (RV.I. 50.6), and in Egyptian mythology, the Sun is the "Eye of Horus."

2 According to the Mihr/Mithra Yasht, the seven regions of the Earth were formed as follows: first came the countries of the rising Sun to the extreme East; then the countries of the setting Sun to the extreme West; two countries to the extreme North, two countries to the extreme South, and in the centre of all these was placed Airyana Vaeja (Iran Vaej), the seed or seat of the Aryans (S.B.E.Vol.XXIII, pp. 122-124; 146).

3 There were Ordeals by Fire and also by Water to prove a man's innocence. The Fire Ordeal consisted in pouring red-hot metal on the bare breast of an individual. If he survived, his innocence was proved. The Ordeal by Water consisted in holding down a man's head under water for some time. If he survived, he was innocent.

4 According to the earliest history of Iran, the Pishdadian, Yima (Vedic Yama), or Jamshid, son of Vivanghvant (Vedic *Vivaswat*), was the third ruler of the world. Under his long reign all things prospered. His sin was two-fold: (a) he permitted the ritual slaughter of the Bull to satisfy the desire of his people to become immortal by eating its consecrated flesh; (b) he was deceived by Angra Mainyu, the Hostile Spirit, and "thereby made eager for supreme sovereignty instead of the service of Ahurmazd." This was the Lie which destroyed him. His Glory *khvarnah* fled from him in the form of a bird, and his creatures perished. He came to a miserable end being sawn in half by the tyrant, Azi Dahak or Zohak (See *Zamyad Yasht*, Yt.19.34-35; *Dadistan-i-Dinik*, xxix, 16-18; S.B.E. Vols. XVII, pp. 418f; XXIII, pp. 293-295). Yima married his sister, Yimak, and the first mortal pair were born from them.

5 Vivanghvant was the father of three sons: Tehmuras, Narsi and Yima, and one daughter, Yimak. Vivanghvant was the first to worship Haoma (Vedic *Soma*) whose juice is drunk in both Zoroastrian and Vedic rituals. As a result of this worship, Yima was born.

6 A pointed reference to the lazy shepherd who neglects to gaze at the Sun to know the time of

day when he should water his pastures at early morn; feed his cattle at high noon; allow them to browse and rest till sunset; and finally, round them up for the night.

7   W.B. Henning asserts that "grehma," taken by several scholars to be the name of a tribe, actually means wealth acquired by looting in Sogdian and Parthian vocabulary. (See W.B. Henning, "The Murder of the Magi," *Journal of the Royal Asiatic Society*, 1944, pp. 133-144; S. Insler, *The Gathas of Zarathushtra*, Acta Iranica, Brill, Leiden, 1975, pp. 207ff).

8   Karapans were the "mumbler" priests who assisted the Zaotar, Chief Priest, at the ritual and the sacrifice. They indulged in drunkenness and corrupt practices.

9   The Kavis were the princelings of Zarathushtra's day. They were also corrupt, with the noble exception of Kavi Vishtaspa, the Prophet's patron. The Kavis were learned in tribal history and legend and skilled in composing mantric verses.

10 *Duraosha*, lit. "keeping death afar," was a term applied to the mythical white Haoma, plant of immortality. Its juice was first extracted and sprinkled on the sacrificial animal, cow, ox, or bull, and the animal roasted on an open fire. Pieces of the roasted meat were then given to each person assembled in the crowd, the priests keeping a portion for themselves. Haoma has been compared to the Ephedra plant from which Ephedrine is extracted. It is also compared to a certain Chinese mushroom whose extract is intoxicating.

Zarathushtra's Dedication: II
Yasna 33
Commentary

The struggle between the Followers of Truth and the Followers of the Lie continues. Zarathushtra, as the enlightened Guide, Ratu, keeps in mind the Primal Laws of Life. He acts as the Judge between the two contenders and tries to be fair to those in whom, Truth and Falsehood are balanced (Ys.33.1).

The Prophet draws together the family, the community and the clan to do their best to bring about a just society (Ys.33.2–4). For this reason he prays that the "most darkened mind" may not overshadow "life's pasture," lit "cow pasture" (Ys.33.4).

Next follows a rare biographical detail. The prophet addresses himself as a Zaotar (Vedic *Zot*), Chief Priest at the ritual (Ys.33.6). He invokes Ahura Mazda to come to him "in essence and in vision" so that he is inspired to work through Truth and the Good Mind. Thus he achieves renown before the Magahood (Ys.33.7). The Magas or Maghavans were learned priests who presided at the religious ceremonies.

He now invokes the blessings of the Twin Powers of Perfection and Immortality who dwell in the dazzling light of Ahura Mazda's Wisdom (Ys.33.9). Everything in the good life belongs to Ahura Mazda who gives us our rewards in keeping with our actions (Ys.33.10). He pleads with Ahura Mazda to have mercy upon him and help him to make a just choice whenever he has to discriminate between good and evil.

The last three verses are considered so important that they are introduced in full in the *Atash Nyaesh*, the prayer in praise of the Holy Fire (Atash), recited daily by the devout. Here Zarathushtra dedicates himself, body and soul, to Ahura Mazda and the fulfilment of his mission on earth. (Ys.33.12–14)

Zarathushtra's Dedication II: Text
Yasna 33

1   The enlightened Guide (Ratu) keeps in mind
    the Primal Laws of Life.
    He will act as judge
    between the Truth-seekers
    and the Followers of the Lie
    and be fair to those
    in whom Truth and Falsehood are balanced.

2   Let man toil with his thought and the actions of both hands
    to frustrate
    the Followers of the Lie.
    Let him lead his fellowmen towards the good.
    He is then in harmony with the Will of Ahura
    and rejoices Mazda.

3   A member of the family, the community or the clan
    should do his best for the righteous.
    He must nourish the living with zeal.
    He will then dwell
    in the lush pastures of Truth and the Good Mind,
    O Ahura.

4   So I will pray away disobedience and evil thought
    from You, O Mazda,
    perversity from the family,
    insidious deceit from the community,
    slanderers from the clan,
    and from life's pasture the most darkened mind.

5   I will now invoke for You and for the Final Goal
    the most mighty Sraosha (willing obedience to Mazda).
    Only then can I gain
    the long-lasting Sovereignty of the Good Mind
    along the straight paths of Truth
    where You, O Ahura Mazda, dwell.

6   I, as Chief Priest (Zaotar),[1]
    call upon Truth that I may fulfil my mission
    towards my followers as You have laid down.
    O Ahura Mazda,
    I strive to see You and take counsel with You
    through Your Supreme Mind.

7   Come to me in essence and in vision O Mazda.
    May I be renowned before the Magahood
    by working through Truth and the Good Mind.
    May the solemn promises made to You
    be understood and fulfilled by us.

8   O Mazda,
    guide my work so that I may continue to worship You
    through the Good Mind.
    I will sing Your praise and cling to Truth.
    Grant me, therefore, the everlasting blessing
    of Your Perfection and Your Immortality.

9   These Twin Powers are Yours, O Mazda.
    They are constant companions of Truth and dwell
    in the dazzling light of Your Wisdom.
    May Your Supreme Mind bless us with these two
    whose souls are united.

10 Everything in the good life is Yours, O Mazda,
    all which has been, which is, and which shall be.
    You give us our rewards
    in keeping with our actions.
    May the vitality in man grow
    through the Good Mind and Truth
    under Your Sovereignty.

11 O Ahura,
    You are the most mighty Lord of Wisdom,
    of Devotion, and Truth which fosters human life.
    It is You
    who nourish the Good Mind and Sovereignty.

Hear my prayer.
Have mercy upon me
whenever there is a reckoning to be made.

12 Arise within me, O Ahura,
and fulfil my ardent desire[2] (for Perfection)
through unflinching Devotion.
O Mazda, Spirit most Holy,
bless me with goodness as a benediction from prayer.
Through Truth confer power:
through the Good Mind, the good reward.

13 O Ahura,
uphold me through Your all-embracing vision.
Reveal to me those fabulous gifts of Your Sovereignty
which are the rewards of the Good Mind.
O radiant Devotion, Armaiti, ·
illumine the consciences of men through Truth.

14 Therefore, Zarathushtra consecrates,
through Rata,[3] the life breath of his person
and the first fruits of his Good Mind to Mazda.
To Truth, he offers his deeds,
his inspired poems,[4] his willing obedience and all the
power
at his command.

Notes

1   Zaotar, Vedic *Zot*, is the name given to the chief officiating priest at the ritual. The Zaotar was highly trained in the recitation and composition of religious verse, understood the symbolic meaning of the ritual performed, and so was honoured by the laity for his spiritual powers (Mary Boyce, "Zoroaster, the Priest" in *Bulletin of the School of Oriental and African Studies*, 33/1 (1970), pp. 22-38; *History of Zoroastrianism*, Brill, Leiden, 1975, Vol.I, p. 183-84).

2   Tevishi (Skt. *Tavishi*) is here used in the sense of ardent desire and not as brutality (Ys.29.1.). See Intro. for explanation.

3   *ratam dadaiti*, in the text. Rata, as Dastur M.N. Dhalla points out, is "the female genius of charity", of unstinted generosity. Zarathushtra's total dedication to Mazda is here being emphasised. See M.N. Dhalla, *Zoroastrian Theology*, New York, 1914, pp. 114-115.

4   Inspired poems, *Ughdha*. In the Avesta there are three grades of human speech: *vacha*, the spoken word of daily speech; *ughdha*, the sublime words of inspired poetry; and the *Manthra Spenta*, the Sacred Word of Power embodied in the Scriptures. Common words can also be raised to embody Truth, as in the phrase, "ba-vacho, Arsh-vacho," those words, those Truth-spoken words.

Zarathushtra's Dedication: III
Yasna 34
Commentary

Zarathushtra's total dedication to Ahura Mazda in thought, word and deed as expressed in the last verse of the previous chapter, is taken up in the opening verse of *Yasna* 34. The reward of this dedication is that Ahura Mazda blesses each individual with Immortality, Truth and the Sovereignty which flows from Perfection (Ys.34.1).

Not only should everyone dedicate himself/herself to Ahura Mazda but all material wealth is to be offered, through prayer, to Ahura Mazda. Thus, no individual can claim anything as his own. His person and his belongings are Ahura Mazda's for ever.

The next verse explains why Fire is held sacred by all believers. This is not physical fire, but Ahura Mazda's Fire, "mighty through Truth," given to the believer for his support. As for those who encourage destruction, this mental Fire will "scorch" them with just "a turn of the hand" (Ys.34.4).

Here again, as in Ys.33.6, we get a glimpse of Zarathushtra's personal attitude to life. He identifies himself with the Drighu, the poor and the downtrodden, who have dared to praise Ahura Mazda above all other divinities in "the presence of false gods and brutish men" (Ys.34.5). He rails bitterly against those who were once initiates but who turn away from his teachings to inflict pain and torture on his followers (Ys.34.7).

He next explains how the Divine Powers interact with each other and with the two warring parties (Ys.34.8-10). Ahura Mazda is the "Remover of Hatred" among those hostile to Him (Ys.34.11). The Path of the Good Mind is the religion of the Saviours, the Saoshyants, who will work towards the Renewal of Existence, the Frashokéréti (Ys.34.13).

In the next verse, a typically Zoroastrian idea is expressed, that of the hamkar or fellow worker. Ahura Mazda invites everyone to place his hand in the hand of the Divine, and together they will bring about the Frashokéréti. Though the word, hamkar, is not found in this verse, Ys.34.14, it is there by implication.

The last verse is the only one in the entire Gathas which the devout are requested to repeat four times to impress upon themselves the need to collaborate with Ahura Mazda for the fulfilment of the entire Creation (Ys.34.15). Thus ends the First Gatha, the Gatha Ahunavaiti, the Gatha of Free Choice.

Zarathushtra's Dedication: III Text
Yasna 34

1 O Mazda, because of that dedicated act,
   that dedicated word, that dedicated worship
   You bless Man
   with Immortality, Truth, and the Sovereignty
   which flows from Perfection. O Ahura,
   may we ever remain Yours and theirs
   the first in our offering (of act, word and worship).

2 You have given all these gifts
   as a reward for the good deeds of the man
   whose soul is united with Truth. O Mazda,
   I will glorify the whole of Your Creation
   with hymns of praise.

3 As a sacrificial offering[1] we dedicate
   all our material wealth and prayer to You,
   O Ahura, and to Your Truth.
   O Mazda,
   these dedications assure for ever, through the Good
   Mind,
   the salvation of the wise counsellor among us.

4 Therefore, O Ahura,
   we long for Your Fire,
   mighty through Truth.
   This enduring flame is offered to the true believer for
   his support.
   But for the destruction-loving,
   this raging flame will scorch him
   with just a turn of the hand.

5 Have You Sovereignty, O Mazda?
   Have You the power to act and protect,
   through Truth and the Good Mind, Your Drighu

such as myself?
We have already dared to praise You above all others
in the presence of false gods and brutish men.

6   O Mazda,
    You are indeed most exalted and powerful
    through Truth and the Good Mind.
    Reveal this as a sign for me to cling to
    amid the uncertainties of life.
    So may I approach You in worship
    and joyous praise.

7   Who are these who were once initiates
    of the Good Mind
    but who now reverse the doctrine and their spiritual
    inheritance
    to inflict pain and torture?. . .
    We know none except You, O Mazda,
    so protect us through Truth.

8   Undoubtedly, these renegades, bring ruin to many
    who terrorise the weak by their actions.
    O Mazda,
    the perverters of Your Doctrines are more formidable
    than Your revilers.
    They will find
    that the Good Mind withdraws far from them
    because they do not honour Your Truth.

9   O Mazda,
    those who perform evil actions through ignorance of
    the Good Mind spurn Your loving Devotion, the
    Beloved of the Wise.
    So she and Truth withdraw
    as far from them as savage beasts of prey withdraw
    from us.

10 But the man of perceptive intellect
    is steadfast in clinging to Truth and the Good Mind.
    Dedicated Devotion is the intimate companion of the
    Good Mind.
    All such revelations come through Your Sovereignty,
    O Ahura Mazda.

11 Thus Your Twin Powers, Perfection and Immortality,
    nourish the soul.
    The Lord's Sovereignty is inherent in the Good Mind.
    This enables Devotion and Truth to increase
    perseverance and moral integrity.
    Through these Powers, O Mazda,
    You are the Remover of Hatred among those hostile to You.

12 What are Your directives?
    What is Your Will?
    How do we praise You?
    How worship?
    Reveal it, O Mazda, for our enlightenment
    so that Your blessings may rest upon us.
    Teach us to follow the path of the Good Mind
    through Truth.

13 This is the path of the Good Mind
    which You, O Mazda, have shown me.
    It is the religion of the Saviours
    whose conduct on earth will be inspired by Truth.
    This will enable the wise to taste of their just reward
    of which You, O Mazda, are the Giver.

14 O Mazda,
    that longed-for reward is indeed given to life
    embodied on earth.
    They who toil to further the well-being of the living
    through the Good Mind are Your collaborators,[2]
    O Ahura.
    They are protected by Truth and reveal
    the divine purpose of Your Wisdom.

15 Hence, O Mazda,
   declare to me the noblest doctrines and finest acts.
   May I proclaim them for Your praise
   through the Good Mind and Truth.
   O Living One, Ahura,
   by Your Power and at Your Will make this life
   renewed.[3]

Notes

1   The word used in the text is *myazda,* ritual offering. Cf Skt *miyédha,* ritual offering.

2   The Avestan word for collaborator is Hamkar, implied but not mentioned in this verse . Every Zoroastrian is expected to place, symbolically, one hand in the hand of Ahura Mazda, and the other in the hand of Asha, the Truth. Together Man and the Divine Powers will work to bring about the Frashokéréti, the wondrous renewal of life, for the entire Creation.

3   This is the only verse in the Gathas which the devout are asked to repeat four times to impress upon themselves the need to work with Ahura Mazda and His Powers to achieve the renewal of our daily life leading finally to the renewal of all life, the Frashokéréti.

Gatha Ushtavaiti:

The Gatha of Supreme Bliss
Zarathushtra Attains Enlightenment
Yasna 43
Commentary

This is the opening chapter of the Second Gatha, the Gatha of Enlightenment and Bliss.

Enlightenment is attained by living the life of the Good Mind. Zarathushtra longs to bring to every man, the ecstatic bliss he has attained. (Ys.43.1).

The man of innate nobility must instruct others concerning the "straight paths of Salvation" bringing together man's body and soul in perfect harmony. These are the paths where Ahura Mazda dwells. As a result, His devotee becomes "resplendent in Wisdom" (Ys.43.3).

Now follow a series of verses opening with the phrase:

> "When the full force of the Good Mind took possession of me,
> O Mazda,
> then I realised You as Mighty and Bountiful."

Ahura Mazda is impartial. He grants their dues to the Truth-seeker and the Follower of the Lie with the same hand through the intensity of His Fire "all powerful through Truth" (Ys.43.4). Spenta Mainyu, The Spirit of Benediction, together with the Good Mind and Sovereignty help the individual to progress in the Truth. Armaiti, heartfelt Devotion, acts as an enlightened guide, instructing each individual in the divine purpose of Ahura Mazda's Wisdom (Ys.43.6).

There comes a dramatic moment when Ahura Mazda Himself, accompanied by His "daughter", Armaiti, speaks to the Prophet encouraging him to place before them his "searching questions" by which he will gain understanding and Sovereignty (Ys.43.10).

Zarathushtra pleads for help for he realises that to do what is best for mankind will cause him suffering (Ys.43.11).

Ahura Mazda ignores the plea, and commands the Prophet in these inspiring words: "Go, instruct man in the Truth and reveal teachings hitherto unheard of..." (Ys.43.12).

Again, one has to bear in mind that Zarathushtra is the first prophet in history to proclaim one, Supreme God, Ahura Mazda, Lord of Life and Wisdom, who demands that each human being *choose* the Truth and live by it. Man must think for himself, choose for himself and follow Truth and the Good Mind in his daily life. He must take responsibility for the consequences of his actions.

Zarathushtra now asserts that Tushnamaiti, silent, meditative thought is the best for man (Ys.43.15). This is the only instance of the word in the Gathas. Unfortunately, nowhere in the extant Avesta is there any description of techiques of meditation.

In the closing verse, Zarathushtra prays: "May Truth incarnate through the power of the life-breath." He chooses for himself Ahura Mazda's Most Bountiful Spirit and reaches out to all mankind with his blessings.

Zarathushtra Attains Enlightenment: Text

Yasna 43

1   Bliss to him who longs for such bliss.[1]
      May Mazda Ahura ruling at will, grant this
      to everyone who desires it.
      O Ahura,
      give me perseverance and moral courage to uphold
      Truth.
      Bestow upon me, through Your loving Devotion,
      that radiant reward...the life of the Good Mind.

2   And so to such a man will be given
      the best of all possessions...bliss.
      By means of Truth and Your Most Bountiful Spirit
      grant, O Mazda, enlightenment
      and the full measure of the Good Mind
      so that each may enjoy unlimited bliss
      all the days of his long life.

3   May that man of innate nobility
      progress from good to greater good.
      May he instruct us
      concerning the straight paths of salvation in this
      bodily life and that of the mind.
      These are the paths
      where Ahura Mazda Himself dwells.
      And so Your ardent devotee
      becomes one like You, O Mazda,
      resplendent in Wisdom.

4   When the full force of the Good Mind took possession
      of me,
      O Mazda,
      then I realised You as Mighty and Bountiful.
      With the same hand You assign their dues
      to the Truth-seekers and the Followers of the Lie

through the intensity of Your Fire, all-powerful
through Truth.

5   Then I realised You as Bountiful, O Mazda Ahura,
     when I saw You as the First at the birth of life.
     Since You maintain that words and deeds bear fruit,
     evil comes to the evil, a good reward to the good
     through the mastery You display
     at the last turning point of existence.[2]

6   To which turning point, O Mazda,
     You will come with Your Spirit of Benediction, Your
     Sovereignty and Your Good Mind
     through whose workings living beings progress in the
     Truth.
     Heartfelt Devotion
     will then act as an enlightened guide (Ratu)
     and instruct them in the divine purpose of Your
     Wisdom
     (both in this world and after death).[3]

7   Then I realised You as Bountiful,
     O Mazda Ahura,
     when the Good Mind encircled me and inquired:
     "Who are you? Whose are you?
     With what divine sign shall I point to the day of
     questioning
     about your life and your person?"[4]

8   Then I answered him:
     "In the first place,
     I am Zarathushtra, the inveterate enemy of the
     Follower of the Lie
     as far as I am able. But to the Follower of Truth
     I would be a powerful support.
     Thus may I attain to glory
     in the desire of Your Sovereignty, O Mazda,
     so long as I praise You and offer my Songs to You."

9   Then I realised You as Bountiful,
    O Mazda Ahura,
    when the Good Mind encircled me.
    His question was:
    "Which party will you claim as your own?"
    Zarathushtra replied:
    "Henceforth, I will consecrate my homage to Your Fire,
    and as long as I am able
    I will meditate upon Your Truth."

10 "Therefore grant me Truth whom I invoke."
    Then Ahura Mazda replied:
    "I come to you with my daughter,
    Armaiti, (full of love and compassion).
    Place before us your searching questions
    for by that questioning you will gain the Sovereignty
    by which you will obtain understanding."

11 Then I realised You as Bountiful,
    O Mazda Ahura,
    when the Good Mind encircled me.
    When I first became enlightened through Your
    inspired Words,
    then I realised
    that to do what is best for mankind
    would cause me suffering.

12 Then You said to me:
    "Go, instruct man in the Truth,
    and reveal teachings hitherto unheard of.
    Hasten towards my Sraosha laden with radiant rewards
    which are the just dues
    of Salvation and Dissolution
    to be distributed among the two contenders."

13 Then I realised You as Bountiful,
O Mazda Ahura,
when the Good Mind encircled me.
Grant me knowledge
of the long-continued desired existence
which none can compel from You,
and which is said to lie in Your Sovereignty.

14 What the initiate is able to give to a friend like me,
O Mazda, grant that enlightened help
by which one may attain Truth.
Let me hasten to overcome
those who despise Your Doctrine,
but be associated with those
who cling to Your Sacred Word.

15 Then I realised You as Bountiful,
O Mazda Ahura,
when the Good Mind encircled me.
He declared that silent meditation[5] is best for man.
Let no man be a great rejoicer of the numerous
Followers of the Lie,
for the Followers of Truth
look upon them all as hostile to You.

16 Thus, O Ahura,
Zarathushtra chooses for himself the Most Bountiful
Spirit which is Yours.
May Truth incarnate through the power of the life-
breath.
May Devotion ever abide with Sovereignty
in sun-like splendour.
May she shower blessings
upon deeds inspired by the Good Mind.

Notes

1 The traditional rendering, based on later interpretations, is: Happiness (ushta) to him who brings utmost happiness to others. Hence the greeting – *ushta-té*, happiness to you.

2 The metaphor is from horse racing referring to the last turn before the winning post is reached. See Ys.51.6.

3 Humbach and Ichaporia, *The Heritage of Zarathushtra* 1994, pp.97, n.5.

4 Rhetorical questions are also common in the Vedas. Insler gives the example: Shall I entreat today for the help of the great gods? (RV.VIII.94. 8ab; Insler, *Gathas*, p. 235).

5 Tushnamaiti, "silent, meditative thought" precedes Armaiti, "perfect thought" according to Pahlavi writers. Tushnamaiti occurs only this once in the Gathas. Compare *tushni-sad*, sitting silently, *Zamyad Yasht* (Yt.19.29), and Vedic *tusnim* seated in silent thought (RV.2-43-4). Tushnamaiti and Armaiti are first names given to Zoroastrian girls to this day. See also Introduction. The opposites of Armaiti are: *Taromaiti*, cussedness, obstinacy; and *Pairimaiti*, devious, roundabout thinking.

Questionings
Yasna 44
Commentary

Yasna 44 is considered the most poetic chapter in the Gathas. Each verse begins with the formula:
"Answer me faithfully that which I ask You, O Ahura."
Very subtly, Zarathushtra gives an answer to each question in the last sentence of each verse.

In the opening verse, Zarathushtra begs Ahura Mazda to teach him how he should venerate Him. The answer is through knowledge gained from the Good Mind and Truth (Ys.44.1). The following verse embodies a very fine definition of Truth (Ys.44.2).

Next follow a series of questions. Who created the Sun and Stars, through whose power does the Moon wax and wane? Who sustains the Earth from below and the Sky from falling from above? Who created light and darkness? Who fashioned dawn, noontide and night? Each questions is linked with a moral issue (Ys.44.3–5).

Zarathushtra now describes how the Divine Powers interact with each other and with every individual. He inquires how he should meditate upon Ahura Mazda's Revelation hidden in His sublime doctrines, and so attain enlightenment (Ys.44.6–10). He realises that from the beginning he was "chosen" by Ahura Mazda to spread abroad His Truth (Ys.44.11).

In subsequent verses Zarathushtra wonders as to how he can expel Untruth from his midst and deliver it into "the hands of Truth". This is to destroy it completely through the sacred words of Ahura Mazda's Teachings (Ys.44.12–14). He questions Ahura Mazda as to who will be victorious in protecting all the living through His Teaching. He then appeals to Ahura Mazda to reveal to him the Healer of Life, the enlightened Guide, Ratu, requesting

Him to let Sraosha (discipline) come to the help of all those struggling to lead a holy life (Ys.44.16). This verse is incorporated in the prayers accompanying the daily ritual of the Kushti.

At this point, Zarathushtra appeals to Ahura Mazda to let his speech grow in power so as to reach Perfection and Immortality through the Sacred Word of Power, the Manthra, which emanates from Truth (Ys.44.17).

Next follows the controversial verse wherein Zarathushtra inquires how he can obtain the promised reward of ten mares, a stallion and a camel so that Perfection and Immortality may be his. This can be explained as a sacramental gift exchange, or, it can be symbolically interpreted through the Bhagvad Gita and the Upanishads (Ys.44.18 n.4).

The chapter concludes with Zarathushtra questioning how the worshippers of Falsehood could ever have been good rulers. He condemns the Karapans, corrupt priests, and the Usiksh, savage tyrants, as well as the Kavis, powerful princelings, for their cruelty to Gaush Urva and her herds (Ys.44.20).

Questionings: Text
Yasna 44

1   Answer me faithfully that which I ask You, O Ahura.
     How shall I venerate one like You, O Mazda?
     Instruct me in this as to a friend.
     May knowledge come to me with the Good Mind and
     Truth
     bringing friendly support.

2   Answer me faithfully that which I ask You, O Ahura.
     Does the wondrous renewal of life yet to come bring
     the best reward of salvation upon the ardent devotee?
     Such a man is indeed blest through Truth,
     the heritage of all, the guardian in spirit,
     the healer of life, the friend, O Mazda.[1]

3   Answer me faithfully that which I ask You, O Ahura.
     Who was the first begetter and father of Truth?
     Who appointed the course of the Sun and Stars?
     Through whose power does the Moon wax and wane?
     I long to know these things and others besides,
     O Mazda.

4   Answer me faithfully that which I ask You, O Ahura.
     Who sustains the earth from below and the sky from
     falling from above?
     Who fashions the Waters and the Plants?
     Who yokes speed to the Wind and the Clouds?
     Who, O Mazda, is the Creator of the Good Mind?

5   Answer me faithfully that which I ask You, O Ahura.
     What wonder-worker wrought the expanses of light
     and the expanses of darkness?
     What wonder-worker created sleep and waking?
     Who fashioned dawn, noontide and night,
     reminders of his duty to the wise man?

6   Answer me faithfully that which I ask You, O Ahura.
If what I declare is true,
then does all-embracing Devotion further Truth
through our actions?
Did You bestow upon mankind
Your Sovereignty through the Good Mind?
For whom have You brought forth this prolific
Joy-giving creation ?[2]

7   Answer me faithfully that which I ask You, O Ahura.
Who created Devotion together with Sovereignty?
Who made the son obedient to the father through
deep insight?
With these questions I strive for enlightenment gained
through Your Benevolent Spirit,
O Mazda, Creator of all.

8   Answer me faithfully that which I ask You, O Ahura.
How shall I meditate upon Your Revelation
hidden in Your sublime Doctrines?
I have learned of them
through Truth and the Good Mind.
What ever-increasing good shall rejoice my soul,
O Mazda?

9   Answer me faithfully that which I ask You, O Ahura.
How shall I maintain in purity my living faith?
Will You, O Mazda,
teach me concerning the ideal Sovereignty?
Only one such as You may dwell in the same realm
with Truth and the Good Mind.

10   Answer me faithfully that which I ask You, O Ahura.
Is Your Revelation the best for all the living?
Does it further
my material well-being together with Truth?
Does it guide my actions justly
through the inspired words of dispassionate
Devotion?

My fervent desire for enlightenment
will surely lead to You, O Mazda.

11   Answer me faithfully that which I ask You, O Ahura.
How shall Devotion be fully possessed
by those to whom Your Revelation has been made?
From the beginning I was chosen by You
to spread abroad Your Truth.
All others I look upon with hostility of
mind.

12   Answer me faithfully that which I ask You, O Ahura.
Who is a Follower of Truth
and who a Follower of the Lie
among those to whom I would preach?
To him who is hostile?
Or, to him who, through evil instruction,
is opposed to Your Salvation?
How shall it be with the one not considered hostile?

13   Answer me faithfully that which I ask You, O Ahura.
How shall I expel untruth from among us?
Those who are full of disobedience
neither shine in the pursuit of Truth
nor delight in the teachings of the Good Mind.

14   Answer me faithfully that which I ask You, O Ahura.
How shall I deliver the Lie into the hands of Truth
to destroy it completely through the Sacred words of
Your Teaching?
Will this cause a mighty split
among the Followers of the Lie
through suffering and strife, O Mazda?

15   Answer me faithfully that which I ask You, O Ahura.
Can You protect me through Truth
when these hostile forces clash together?
Upon which of the two
will You grant the victory

by means of Your Foreknowledge, O Mazda?

16 Answer me faithfully that which I ask You, O Ahura.
Who will be victorious
in protecting all the living with Your Teaching?
Reveal to me the Healer of Life, the enlightened Guide.
Then let Sraosha (discipline) come to him with the
Good Mind,
to whomsoever You will, O Mazda.[3]

17 Answer me faithfully that which I ask You, O Ahura.
How shall I,
working in harmony with You,
create a close fellowship devoted to Your Will?
Let my speech grow in power
to reach up to Perfection and Immortality
through that Sacred Word, the Manthra,
which emanates from Truth.

18 Answer me faithfully that which I ask You, O Ahura.
How may I obtain, through Truth,
that promised reward,
namely, ten mares, a stallion and a camel,
so that Perfection and Immortality may be mine, O Mazda?[4]

19 Answer me faithfully that which I ask You, O Ahura.
He who withholds the prize from one justly deserving it
in fulfilment of our promise,
what will be his punishment here and now?
I am aware of that which shall come to him in the end.

20 How, O Mazda,
could the Daeva-worshippers ever have been good rulers?
I ask this
on behalf of those whom the Karapan and the Usiksh[5]
have oppressed,
delivering the herds to Wrath.
The Kavis too are cruel to Gaush Urva
causing her constant pain and misery.

Nor do they approach Truth
to cultivate pastures for her well-being.

Notes

1   Personal interpretation.

2   Lit. the joy-giving Cow. Here and
in Ys.47-2. the Cow represents the
whole of Creation.

3   This verse is incorporated in the
Kemna Mazda prayer which
accompanies the daily ritual of
the Kushti.

4   Humbach considers the "material
reward" as the "fee" expected
from the laity by the Zaotar, chief
officiating priest at the ritual.
Irach J.S. Taraporewala, in a
personal communication, insists
that Zarathushtra is here offering
Ahura Mazda his total self
consisting of: his ten senses, five
of action and five of inaction (ten
mares) his mind (stallion); and
his faith (camel), held by
C.G. Jung as a Zoroastrian

archetype of the Good Religion.
This verse is a classic example of
the sacramental gift exchange
when a devotee offers both his
mental and his material gifts to
Ahura Mazda in return for the
rewards of Perfection and
Immortality. (See Katha
Upanishad, III, 3-5; R.E. Hume, *The
Thirteen Principal Upanishads*,
Oxford, 1921, p. 351; also
Bhagvatgita, XIII, 5.)

5   Usiksh is mentioned this once in
the entire Avesta and has been
compared with the Vedic *Usig*, a
family of priests who first
established the worship of Agni
(Fire). So Agni is called "the Usig
of the gods" in the Vedas. (S.B.E.
XLVI, pp. 52ff; 233, 297).

The Twin Mentalities
and The Sacred Word
Yasna 45
Commentary

In Yasna 43.12, Ahura Mazda had commanded Zarathushtra to instruct mankind in the Truth and reveal teachings hitherto unheard of. In Yasna 45 Zarathushtra takes up the challenge. Each verse begins with an emphatic: "I declare this to you". He is addressing a crowd "from near and afar" on the need to follow the Sacred Word he preaches. He warns the people against false teachers and Followers of the Lie who mislead with their speech (Ys.45.1).

He then deliberately alludes to the Twin Mainyu explained in Ys.30, and summarises their differences. The Twin Mentalities are in opposition in thought, doctrine, in directive intelligence, in their preferences, in words, deeds, consciences and souls (Ys.45.2).

He warns his audience that whoever refuses to practise the Sacred Word, the Manthra, as he explains it, will suffer in this present life (Ys.45.3).

He declares that Ahura Mazda has established the best life in harmony with Truth, for He is the Father of the Good Mind, and His daughter is Armaiti, Devotion, nourisher of good deeds. Unless man performs good deeds with love and devotion he cannot lead the good life for the all-seeing Ahura cannot be deceived (Ys.45.4).

Zarathushtra now explains the results which follow when man practises the Sacred Word. He will advance towards Perfection and Immortality for Ahura Mazda is the "Lord of actions inspired by the Good Mind" (Ys.45.5). He pours out His blessings on every thing that lives (Ys.45.6).

All creatures long for the Salvation (Sava) Ahura Mazda offers. The souls of the just dwell in Immortality, while the torments of the wicked endure (Ys.45.7).

In the concluding verses, Zarathushtra magnifies Ahura Mazda in prayers of intense devotion. In the final verse he alludes to the Saviours, the Saoshyants, who protect the Holy Revelation and look upon Ahura Mazda as the Master of the House, a Brother, nay Father (Ys.45.8–11).

The Twin Mentalities and The Sacred Word: Text
Yasna 45

1   I declare this to you.
     Be attentive.
     Listen, both you who from near and you who from afar
     have yearned to know.
     Keep these doctrines clearly in mind.
     The false prophet can never destroy life a second time
     even though the Follower of the Lie,
     through his evil preference, chooses to mislead with
     his tongue.

2   I declare this to you.
     It concerns the two Primal Spirits, twins,
     of whom the more benevolent addressed the hostile
     one:
     "Neither our thoughts, nor doctrines,
     nor directive intelligence, nor preferences,
     neither words nor deeds,
     neither consciences nor souls agree."

3   I declare this to you
     about the first life[1] about which Ahura Mazda has
     spoken.
     Whoever among you
     will not practise this Sacred Word
     as I conceive and voice it,
     for him this present life will be woe.

4   I declare this to you.
     Mazda, who knows all things,
     has established the best life in harmony with Truth.
     He is the Father of the empowering Good Mind,
     and His daughter is Armaiti (Devotion)
     nourisher of good deeds.
     Not to be deceived is the all-seeing Ahura.

5   I declare to you
    what the Most Benevolent One said to me:
    "My Word is the best for mortals to hear.
    They who will offer willing obedience to My Word
    will advance towards Perfection and Immortality.
    Mazda is the Lord of actions inspired by the Good
    Mind."

6   I now declare to you
    the most glorious of all,
    praising, through Truth, Him who pours out His
    blessings on every thing that lives.
    May Mazda Ahura be gracious to me
    through His Benevolent Spirit in whose adoration
    the Good Mind has guided me.
    May He, in His Wisdom, teach me of the highest.

7   Indeed,
    all those who are, who were, who shall be,
    long for the salvation He offers.
    The souls of the just dwell in Immortality
    while the torments of the wicked endure.
    Mazda Himself is the Creator of these principles
    through His Sovereignty.

8   I will praise Him with hymns of adoration.
    As an initiate,
    I see Him clearly in my mind's eye through Truth.
    He is the Lord of word and deed
    through the Good Mind.
    We offer Him our prayers
    to be treasured in His House of Song.

9   I will rejoice Him
    together with the Good Mind for our sake.
    He creates for us both fortune and misfortune at will.
    May Mazda Ahura, by means of His Sovereignty,
    grant us strength
    to prosper our cattle and men[2]

through our association with
Truth and the Good Mind.

10   I will magnify Him
with prayers of intense Devotion
for He is ever addressed as Mazda Ahura.
He has assigned to man Perfection and Immortality
in His Kingdom through Truth and the Good Mind.
May they bless us with moral courage and
perseverance.

11   Whoever among these Daevas (false gods),
and inferior men may be,
they are different from those who revere Ahura.
These are the enlightened Saviours,
protecting the Holy Revelation.
Mazda Ahura is to them
both Master of the House and Friend.
He is like a Brother, nay Father.[3]

Notes

1   The First life refers to the primeval life of perfection which existed before Angra Mainyu, the Hostile Spirit, attacked Ahura Mazda's perfect creation. The Frashokéréti will bring back this Renewal of Existence at the end of Time.

2   See Ys.31.15, n.4.

3   Personal interpretation.

Zarathushtra's Trials

Yasna 46
Commentary

In the previous chapter Zarathushtra made his dynamic appeal urging the people to turn to Truth and the Good Mind, study the Manthra, the Sacred Word, and do good deeds in the name of Ahura Mazda, the one Supreme God of Truth and Justice. Naturally, the Kavis and the Karapans feel threatened. They terrorise the peasants and the cultivators into abject submission. The Prophet is hounded from village to village. His plight is depicted in the first two verses (Ys.46.1 and 2).

Zarathusthra, however, stands firm in his mission. "The glittering, dawing of the days" *Ukshano āsnām*, will herald the coming of the Saoshyants who will bring about the Renewal of Existence. The Prophet appeals to the Good Mind for inspiration. The Vedic links with the phrase *Ukshano āsnām* are fully explained. (Ys.46.3 n.1).

He rails against the Followers of the Lie and those who mislead others. He points out that he is holy to whom the Follower of Truth is a friend. It is man's Daena, his conscience, that perceives this (Ys.46.4-6).

The next verse is familiar to all Zoroastrians as it opens the daily ritual of the Kushti prayers. Zarathushtra questions as to who will be his protector when the Follower of the Lie threatens him with violence. He answers his own question: "Who other than Your Fire and Your mind through whose actions Truth is fulfilled?" (Ys.46.7).

Zarathushtra is a firm believer in the equality of the sexes. He boldly asserts: "Forth with them all (man or woman) will I cross the Bridge of Judgement ." (Ys.46.10). He accuses the Kavis and the Karapans of "yoking mankind to the destruction of life."

Yet, their "own souls and evil conscience will torment them when they reach the Bridge of Judgement." (Ys.46.11).

In the succeeding verses Zarathushtra praises those who have joined the new faith. He begins with the exceptional Turanians who are friendly to the new faith (Ys.46.12). He then invokes his patron, Kavi Vishtaspa, his own family members, the Haechataspan Spitamas, and lastly, the two brothers, Frashaoshtra and Jamaspa, senior ministers at the Court of Vishtaspa (Ys.46.15-17).

He concludes by asserting that he who helps him in his work through Truth will receive the reward of the "best existence" after death, while in this life he will be filled with abundance. Ahura Mazda is the "greatest Giver of such gifts," (Ys.46.19).

Zarathushtra's Trials: Text
Yasna 46

1   To what land shall I flee? Where can I turn for refuge?
They have excluded me from family and clan.
Nor does the community seek to rejoice me,
nor by any chance, the wicked despots of the land.
How then can I rejoice You,
O Mazda Ahura?

2   I know that by which I am helpless, O Mazda.
Mine is a scanty herd, and my followers are few.
So I cry to You, see to it, O Ahura,
for I ask for that support
which the Heavenly Friend grants to his earthly friend.
Teach me through Truth
concerning the riches of the Good Mind.

3   When, O Mazda,
will those who herald the glittering dawning of the days[1]
come forward to uphold the Truth-inspired existence[2]
by means of the guiding intellect of the Saviours?
To whom will the Good Mind come for inspiration?
To me,
O Ahura,
for I am chosen by You for its fulfilment.

4   Thus does the Follower of the Lie
Prevent those who support Truth
from furthering the progress of our cattle in province
or country.
He is an invoker of evil
defrauding the people by his repellent actions.
Whoever deprives him of vital power, O Mazda,
that individual shall lead mankind
along the paths of the Good Chisti (to
enlightenment).

5   Such a man
is well versed in commitments and duties.
He is a Follower of Truth
empowered to secure one coming to him for
enlightenment.
He will impart a living integrity to this Follower of the Lie.
Being discerning,
he will claim this fallen one as his kinsman,
keeping him from bloodshed,
O Mazda Ahura.

6   But the man who does not desire
to come to him for enlightenment
will surely fall among the companions of the Lie.
For he is holy
to whom the Follower of the Truth is a friend.
It has ever been thus
since You first created consciences in men, O Mazda.

7   O Mazda,
whom have You appointed as protector over me
when the Follower of the Lie threatens me with violence?
Who other than Your Fire
and Your Mind through whose actions Truth is fulfilled,
O Ahura?
Declare to my conscience this sacred doctrine.[3]

8   May he who is determined upon harassing my
followers not afflict us by his actions.
May these redound upon him
with the virulence
which has kept him from the good life.
That very hostility keeps him bound to the evil life,
O Mazda.

9   Who is he, the foremost devotee,
who will teach me
how we may glorify You as the Most Bountiful,
as radiant in action, Lord of Life and Truth?

Whatever is Yours through Truth,
whatever the Creator of Cattle, Gaush Tasha,
has declared to Truth,
with these all men will question me through
the Good Mind.

10 O Mazda Ahura,
that man or woman who gives to me the life
which You know to be the best,
will receive the blessings of Truth and Your
Sovereignty through the Good Mind.
And those whom I shall draw towards Your adoration,
forth with them all (man or woman),
will I cross the Bridge of Judgement.

11 The Karapans and the Kavis,
through their domination and evil deeds,
have yoked mankind to the destruction of life.
Their own souls and evil consciences
will torment them when they reach
the Bridge of Judgement.
They will remain in the House of the Lie for ever.

12 (The day will come) when, from among the noble
offspring of the Turanian Freyana,[4]
there will arise those who further life
through their zeal
for Devotion and Truth.
Then Ahura Mazda will unite them to the Good Mind
and manifest Himself among them for their support.

13 That man will be renowned as upright
who seeks to rejoice Spitama Zarathushtra by his zeal.
Mazda Ahura will further his spiritual life,
increase his possessions through the Good Mind,
and reveal Himself as a Friend through Truth.

14 O Zarathushtra, who is your righteous ally
who wants to be renowned

for taking part in the great Sacrament?
Indeed, he is the valiant Kavi Vishtaspa himself.
In the words of the Good Mind,
I will invite those whom You have established
in Your Kingdom.

15 O descendants of the Haechataspan Spitamas,[5]
to you I will proclaim . . . .
so that you may discriminate between the wise and
the unwise. Truth belongs to you
through actions which are in keeping
with the Primal Laws of Ahura.

16 O Frashaoshtra Hvogva,
come, join the faithful
with those for whom we both wish this life's blessings:
blessings where Perfect Devotion blends with Truth,
where the desirable Kingdom of the Good Mind is found,
where the Lord of Life and Wisdom abides
in the Heaven of His bounty.

17 Since I declaim in measured verse
and not in non-verse,[6]
O Jamaspa Hvogva,
therefore invoke Sraosha (inspiration) for your
understanding.
Thus may you discriminate
between the law-abiding and the breakers of the law
through the wise counsellor and through Truth
which belongs to Mazda Ahura.

18 Whoever is loyal to me,
I promise him the highest award through the Good Mind.
Afflictions upon him
who would deliver us to wickedness.
O Mazda,
I seek but to fulfil Your Will through Truth.
Such is the perception of my understanding and intellect.

19 Whoever will accomplish for me, Zarathushtra,
   my most cherished desire through Truth,
   he will most deservedly receive the reward
   of the best existence at death.
   And in this life he will be filled with abundance.[7]
   You are the greatest Giver of such gifts, O Mazda.

Notes

1 *Ukshano āsnām,* the Bulls of the Heavens. Cf. Ys.44.5; 50.10. This is a Vedic image. "Protect the cherished tracks of the cows of dawn . . . This is the great face of the great (gods) which, leading, the cows of dawn shall follow" (RV.I.67-5-6-9). Humbach translates as "the light of the Sun," Uksha as the "Bulls of the days." (See Humbach, *Gathas,* II, pp. 177, 220.) Duchesne-Guillemin translates as "the dawns of the days" (Duchesne-Guillemin, *The Hymns of Zarathushtra,* p. 75. See also Harvey P. Alper, *Mantra,* Albany, N.Y. 1987, pp. 21, 37).

2 Referring to the "first life" which existed before Angra Mainyu, the Hostile Spirit, poisoned existence.

3 This verse is included in the Kemna Mazda prayer recited in the daily ritual of the winding and unwinding of the sacred thread, the Kushti.

4 The marauding border tribe of the Tuira/Tura (Iraq) were in constant warfare with the Iranian villagers, but one tribe, the Freyana, were friendly. (See Richard N. Frye, *The History of Ancient Iran,* Munich, 1984, pp. 51, 60.)

5 Haechataspa was the fourth, and Spitama the ninth ancestor of the Prophet according to Pahlavi tradition.

6 "afshmani noit anafshmani," variously translated. Insler, "in verse, not in non-verse" (op.cit., p. 85); Kellens and Pirart, "in verse, not in prose" (*Les Textes veils Avestique,* Vol.I, p. 163); Humbach, "duties not non-duties" (*op.cit.,*II,p. 187); Duchesne-Guillemin, "I will recall only your merits and not your faults" (*op.cit.,* p. 83); I.J.S. Taraporewala, "in action, not in inaction," *Divine Songs of Zarathushtra The Gathas, a Philological Study,* Bombay, 1951, pp. 629-630).

7 Lit. *gava azi,* cows-in-calf.

Gatha Spenta Mainyu:
The Gatha of The Sacred Spirit
Yasna 47
Commentary

We now come to the Gatha Spenta Mainyu, Ahura Mazda's ever-expanding Spirit of Benediction. The first verse of Yasna 47 invokes all the Divine Powers. The Good Mind, being a part of the Supreme Mind of Ahura Mazda, is not mentioned by name. Zarathushtra reaffirms his faith that Perfection and Immortality will come to whoever dedicates his life in thought, word and deed to the Divine Powers (Ys.47.1).

The second verse emphasizes that every man can cultivate the best life by working hand in hand with the Spirit of Benediction, by speaking with the "mouth and tongue" of the Good Mind, and by performing good deeds "by the hands of Devotion." This unique insight reveals to the Prophet that Ahura Mazda is the "Father of Truth" (Ys.47.2).

Not only is Ahura Mazda the Father of Truth, He is also the Father of Spenta Mainyu "who moulded this joyous Creation", lit. the "joy-giving Cow." Here the Cow symbolises the whole of Creation, for the Spirit of Benevolence pervades the entire Universe and does not limit itself to the animal kingdom (Ys.47.3 Cf 44.6). The wicked, recoil from this Bountiful Spirit, but the Followers of Truth do not. The former are their own greatest enemies for they enjoy the fruits of their own actions which stem from the Evil Mind (Ys.47.4 and 5).

In the concluding verse Zarathushtra once again asserts that Ahura Mazda distributes their just dues to both the Truth-seekers and to the Followers of the Lie. It is Ahura Mazda's justice that will draw to Himself all seekers "sustained by Devotion and Truth" (Ys.47.6).

The Gatha of the Sacred Spirit: Text
Yasna 47

1   Through Your Spirit of Benediction
and Your Supreme Mind
You will grant Perfection and Immortality to him
whose words and deeds are in harmony with Truth,
with the Sovereignty of Mazda
and the Devotion of Ahura.

2   Through this Most Benevolent Spirit
the best life will be cultivated by him
who speaks with the words from the mouth and
tongue of the Good Mind,
and whose actions are performed
by the hands of Devotion.
This unique insight reveals
Mazda as the Father of Truth.

3   You are indeed the Father
of this life-enhancing Spirit
who moulded this joyous creation.
So to the caring herdsman is given
the peace of Devotion so that he may take counsel
with the Good Mind, O Mazda.

4   The wicked recoil from this Spirit
benevolent through Mazda.
But the Followers of Truth do not.
Whether possessing little or much,
let man be generous to the righteous,
but hostile to the wicked.

5   O Mazda Ahura,
through that Spirit of Benediction You promise all that
is best
to the Follower of Truth.

The Follower of the Lie,
without Your approval, enjoys the fruits
of his own actions which stem from the Evil Mind.

6   O Mazda Ahura,
You distribute their just dues to the two contenders
through Your Spirit of Benediction
and Your Fire.
This shall indeed
convert the many who are seekers
sustained by Devotion and Truth.

The Conquest of The Lie: I
Yasna 48
Commentary

Having invoked all the Divine Powers in the previous chapter, Zarathushtra returns to the perennial theme of the Gathas, the conquest of the Lie by the Truth, resulting in the just overcoming the wicked (Ys.48.1–2).

In the next two verses Zarathushtra declares how the initiate receives the best of doctrines and acts upon them while Ahura Mazda assigns "a distinct place" to those who follow their own inclinations according to their conscience (Ys.48.3 and 4).

Zarathushtra now addresses Armaiti, loving Devotion, to let good rulers rule through penetrating insight. She Armaiti, is the "Treasured One of the Good Mind". Hence, for her sake Ahura Mazda made plants flourish at the birth of primeval life (Ys.48.5–6).

Zarathushtra does not mince his words in condemning Wrath and Cruelty. He constantly asks how one may strive to establish good rule among the people. He longs for the future Saviour, Saoshyant, to come so that man may recognise the message of Salvation (Ys.48.7–9).

In Ys.48.10, Zarathushtra refers to "this filth of a drink" by which the corrupt priests, the Karapans, delude the Kavis, evil rulers, by intoxicating them with the juice of the Haoma, Vedic *soma*, plant.

In the last two verses Zarathushtra appeals once again to Armaiti to give the community good shelter and rich pasturage. He also addresses the Saoshyants as "the Saviours of the Lands" and begs them to fulfil Ahura Mazda's teachings and so destroy Wrath (Ys.48.11–12).

The Conquest of the Lie: I
Yasna 48

1   The wicked shall be overpowered
     and Truth conquer the Lie
     as preordained at the Final Judgement
     destined from the beginning
     for men and the Followers of the Lie for ever.
     So Your promise of Salvation
     will increase our adoration of You,
     O Ahura.

2   Tell me, O Ahura,
     You who know these things,
     what will occur even before the Final Judgement?
     When will the just overcome the wicked, O Mazda?
     Then indeed
     will come about the wondrous renewal of life.

3   The initiate receives the best of doctrines
     which Ahura, the Giver of Good,
     teaches through Truth. You, the Benevolent One,
     reveal the most profound teachings[1]
     which are Your very own:
     these which exist in the wisdom of the Good Mind,
     O Mazda.

4   In Your Wisdom, O Mazda,
     You will assign a distinct place to the man
     who, for better or for worse,
     follows in word and deed his own inclinations,
     desires and beliefs according to his conscience.

5   Let good rulers rule over us
     through actions inspired by penetrating insight,
     O Armaiti
     Let not wicked rulers rule over us.

Purity from birth is best for man.
Let the herdsman vitalize the cow/ox and thus produce
abundant food for mankind[2].

6   She (Armaiti) gives us good shelter,
perseverance and endurance,
she, the Treasured One[3] of the Good Mind.
Hence, for her sake Mazda Ahura,
through Truth,
made plants flourish at the birth of primeval life.

7   Down with Wrath!
Crush cruelty,
you who would maintain, through Truth,
the widespread penetration of the Good Mind
in whose company walks the just man.
Such dwell in Your House of Song, O Ahura.

8   How, O Mazda, may one strive for Your good rule?
What will be Your reward for me, O Ahura?
Which of Your ardent devotees do I seek out through Truth
so that I may further the actions of the Good Mind?

9   When will I know
if You have Sovereignty, through Truth,
over those whose hostility threatens me, O Mazda?
May the sublime words
befitting the Good Mind be rightly uttered by me.
Let the Future Saviour know
what his reward in this life will be.

10   When, O Mazda,
will men recognise the message of Salvation?
When will they remove this filth of a drink[4]
by which these hostile Karapans, through their
perverse intellect,
cause intoxication and so delude the evil rulers of
these lands?

11 When O Mazda,
    will Your loving Devotion, Armaiti,
    in harmony with Truth,
    give us good shelter and rich pasturage through Your
    Sovereignty?
    Who will establish peace for us
    from the blood-thirsty wicked?
    To whom will the penetrating insight of the Good Mind
    come?

12 Indeed, they will be the Saviours of the Lands
    working through the Good Mind
    and performing deeds in harmony with Truth.
    They will strive
    for the fulfilment of Your Teachings, O Mazda.
    Such men are destined to be the destroyers of Wrath.

Notes

1   The phrase, Guzra Sengha,
    profound teachings, is usually
    translated as "secret doctrines."
    Throughout the Gathas,
    Zarathushtra speaks both at the
    literal and metaphoric level.
    Hence, Guzra Sengha would
    signify profound doctrines rather
    than any secret teachings
    Zarathushtra wished to hide
    from his listeners.

2   Cf. Duchesne-Guillemin, "let the
    ox grow fat for our nourishment"
    (*op.cit.* p. 37), and M.W. Smith,
    "Fatten her for our food" (*op.cit.*,
    p. 134).

3   Cf. M.W. Smith–she, "the treasure
    of good purpose" (*op.cit*, p. 135)
    and Duchesne-Guillemin, "She,
    the consecrated of the Good
    Mind" (*op.cit*, p. 37).

4   Referring to the juice of the
    Haoma plant used in both Vedic
    and Zoroastrian rituals to this
    day. When drunk in excess by the
    Karapans, "mumbler" priests, it
    caused drunkenness and racking
    pain. (See Humbach, *Gathas*, II,
    p. 208).

The Conquest of The Lie: II
Yasna 49
Commentary

In this chapter also, as in the previous one, Zarathushtra continues to fight against his persecutors. He singles out the Bendva chief "of evil intent" as inflicting utmost harm upon him because he befriended the oppressed and tried to get justice due to them. In the next verse also the Bendva is again mentioned. These are the only instances in the entire Avesta where the word occurs (Ys.49.1–2).

The Prophet clings all the more closely to Truth "which is given us for our choice, the support of our faith and the destruction of wickedness." He condemns those who through their evil intellect "increase Wrath and Cruelty with their tongue." Such men have planted "false Gods in the conscience of the Followers of the Lie" (Ys.49.3–4).

On the other hand, the just man unites his conscience with the Good Mind and so increases Ahura Mazda's power. Such an individual, being rooted in Devotion and Truth, will obtain Sovereignty over all things through Ahura Mazda. Ultimately, Evil can never triumph (Ys.49.5).

In the following five verses Zarathushtra urges Ahura Mazda to reveal the Divine purpose of His Wisdom for our just choice. He begs for the joyous companionship of Truth for himself and his friend, Frashaoshtra, a minister at the Court of Vishtaspa, his patron. He places all the souls of the righteous in Ahura Mazda's House of Song, that is, in Bliss (Ys.49.6–10).

He then prophesies that all evil rulers, evil speakers, evil thinkers and those of evil conscience will fall headlong into the House of the Lie where the condemned souls will receive them with "foul food" (Ys.49.11). In the last verse, He dedicates himself once again to Ahura Mazda (Ys.49.12).

The Conquest of the Lie: II Text
Yasna 49

1 Thus has this Bendva[1], of evil intent,
   long since oppressed me
   because I tried to help the downtrodden through Justice
   due to them.
   O Mazda,
   come to me as a great blessing.
   Help me.
   Grant me the power
   to conquer this Bendva's destructiveness
   through the Good Mind.

2 But the lying creed of this Bendva
   keeps me from this work –
   deceiver that he is and far removed from the Truth.
   He does not strengthen benevolent Devotion in this
   life,
   nor does he commune with the Good Mind,
   O Mazda.

3 For this reason, O Mazda,
   Truth is given us for our choice,
   the support of our faith, and the destruction of
   wickedness.
   Therefore I long
   to be united with the Good Mind and renounce
   all the Followers of the Lie and their associates.

4 They who through their perverse intellect
   increase Wrath and Cruelty with their tongue –
   the non-herdsmen among the herdsmen –
   these are the evildoers
   whose desire is not towards good deeds.
   They have established false gods
   in the conscience of the Followers of the Lie.

5   But the man who unites his conscience
     with the Good Mind is both zealous and increases
     Your Power,
     O Mazda.
     Being rooted in Devotion and Truth
     he will obtain Sovereignty over all things
     through You, O Ahura.

6   So now I urge You,
     O Mazda, and you, O Truth,
     to reveal the divine purpose of Your Wisdom for our
     just choice.
     Let us honour the conscience
     planted in Your Followers, O Ahura.

7   Let every man hear of Your Doctrine through the Good
     Mind, O Mazda, and let him hear of it through Truth.
     Turn to me, O Ahura.
     Who will be the friend and who the member of the
     clan
     who will bring good repute to the community by these
     Laws?

8   May you grant the joyous companionship of Truth to
     Frashaoshtra.
     This I beseech You, O Ahura Mazda,
     and to me also.
     May we be at all times Your angelic messengers[2]
     revealing Your Sovereign Good.

9   Let the Zealous reformer listen
     to Your Sacred Doctrines.
     Let not the Truth-speaker join
     with the Follower of the lie.
     Those who unite their conscience with Truth
     Will receive the highest award
     On the Day of Judgement,
     O Wise Jamaspa.

10   And these, O Mazda,
     I will place in Your House of Song –
     the Good Mind and the souls of the just,
     together with our homage to Devotion.
     May You strengthen these
     with the might of Your Sovereignty.

11   But evil rulers, evil doers, evil speakers,
     those of evil conscience and evil thinkers,
     such wicked ones will fall headlong into the House of
     the Lie.
     There the souls will receive them
     with foul food, and there their comradeship will be.

12   What help can be had
     through Truth and the Good Mind for Your invoker,
     O Ahura Mazda? Who will rejoice You with songs of
     praise
     beseeching for that which is Your Sovereign Desire?

Notes

1   The Bendva chief mentioned in
    Ys.49.1 and 2 are the only
    references to this name in the
    entire Avesta. Geldner interprets
    the word as "defiler" and
    considers it an accusation
    against Zarathushtra by his
    enemies (Insler, *Gathas*, p. 296).

2   *Farishta*, i.e. Angelic Powers.
    "Farishta" is still in common use.

Zarathushtra Communes with The Divine Powers

Yasna 50
Commentary

This chapter reveals Zarathushtra in communion with Ahura Mazda. Zarathushtra is utterly disillusioned with the people among whom he lives and works. He turns for support to Ahura Mazda, His Supreme Mind and Truth (Ys.50.1). He invokes Wisdom and its followers, Truth, the Supreme Mind and Sovereignty. The Seekers after Truth behold "the Sun (of Wisdom)" and are firmly set upon their path by listening to the voice of Sraosha, who, in this context, symbolises willing obedience to Ahura   Mazda (Ys.50.2–4).

For the second time in the Gathas Zarathushtra refers to himself as a Manthran, a reciter and preacher of the Manthra, the Sacred Word of Power. The Manthran not only heals through prayer, but has visionary insight into what will or will not be (Ys.50.5; Cf Ys.31.5, and 32.13).

Zarathushtra now addresses Ahura Mazda as the Creator, the Charioteer, to whom he will yoke "the swiftest of Steeds, far reaching in victorious prayer, strong through Truth and the Good Mind", racing towards the fulfilment of life, the Frashokéréti the "wondrous renewal of existence" (Ys.50.6–7).

Not only does Zarathushtra adore Ahura Mazda "with outstretched hands", but he again mentions the coming of the future Saviours of the World (Ys.50.8 and 10; Cf 46.3 n.1)

The chapter concludes with a heartfelt appeal to Ahura Mazda by the Prophet to hasten the fulfilment of life, the Frashokéréti (Ys.50.11 Cf.46.3; and 44.5)

Zarathushtra Communes with the Divine Powers: Text

Yasna 50

1   What help can my soul depend upon and from whom?
     Who is the protector of me and my herds?
     Who other than Truth,
     and You, O Mazda Ahura, most invoked,
     and Your Supreme Mind?

2   How may one who desires abundant herds in this life
     seek the best of nourishing pastures?
     The rightly living who follow Truth
     are among those who behold the Sun (of Wisdom).[1]
     Indeed, You will give them a distinct place
     among the wise ones.

3   Wisdom will come to them with Truth,
     the Good Mind and the promised Sovereignty.
     Whoever retrieves and prospers for us
     the neighbouring settlements which the Followers of
     the Lie have annexed,
     he shall receive the empowering reward of that
     Sovereignty.

4   O Mazda Ahura,
     thus with hymns of praise I will worship You,
     with Truth, the Supreme Mind and Your Sovereignty.
     The seeker after Truth is firmly set upon his path
     by listening to the voice of Sraosha (willing obedience
     to Mazda),
     which leads those worthy
     to the House of Song.

5   I will strive to be
     Your devotee through Truth, O Mazda Ahura.
     You favour Your Manthra-preacher, Zarathushtra,

with visible and far-reaching support,
beckoning to all to dwell in bliss.

6   This Manthra-reciter, Zarathushtra,
    who raises his voice in reverence, is an ally of Truth.
    May the Creator, as Charioteer,
    teach me how to follow the directives of the Good Mind
    by guiding the path of my tongue
    through His Wisdom.

7   So I will yoke for You, O Mazda,
    the swiftest of steeds,[2]
    far-reaching in victorious prayer, strong through Truth
    and the Good Mind.
    May You race ahead (towards the Fraskokéréti).
    Be there my help.[3]

8   With hands outstretched in adoration,
    and with fervent prayer in measured verse welling up
    from my heart,
    I would encircle You, O Mazda,
    and you, O Truth, and you, O Good Mind,
    skilled in virtue, for I am one of the faithful.

9   With songs of praise may I ever come into Your
    presence, O Mazda,
    through Truth and the Good Mind's actions.
    So long as I rule over my desire at will,
    I shall strive to follow
    in the footsteps of the wise counsellor.

10 Thus whatever acts I may perform in the future,
    and whatever deeds were performed in the past,
    and whatever is precious in the eyes of the Good
    Mind –
    such as the light of the Sun, the glittering dawning of
    the days[4] –
    these are for
    Your praise and adoration through Truth,

O Mazda Ahura.

11 So I will call myself a singer of Your praise,
O Mazda,
and be one as long as I work through Truth.
May the Creator of life
lead us through the Good Mind
to that fulfilment of existence (the Frashokéréti) which
we long for.

Notes

1 See Ys.32.2, n.1.

2 The horse as a symbol of prayer
is depicted on a Sasanian seal in
the British Museum, London. On
one side of the seal is the head of
a king. On the other, an Afarghan
or fire altar, in which are seen
leaping flames. In the centre of
the flames, is a horse, forelegs
raised, symbol of ascending
prayer.

3 See Insler, *Gathas*, p. 308.

4 See Ys.46.3, n.1. Cf.Ys.44.5.

Gatha Vohu Khashathra:

The Gatha of Divine Sovereignty;
Striving Towards the Spiritual Goal
Yasna 51
Commentary

The Fourth Gatha, the Gatha of the Good Kingdom, the Good Sovereignty, consists of just one chapter of twenty-two verses. Zarathushtra never wavers from his mission. He appeals to all men to cling to the blessings of Ahura Mazda's Salvation achieved by following the Good Mind (Ys.51.1–3).

Zarathushtra, after all, is very human. The next verse is a cry from in heart. But his determination never wavers. Again, he refers to the impartiality of Ahura Mazda towards the Seekers after Truth and the Followers of the Lie. Both parties will be tested by Ahura Mazda's "blazing Fire" within each individual, and by the ordeal of molten metal (Ys.51.9).

An incident in his life is revealed in Ys.51.12. He is bitter against the sodomite Kavi who refused to give him and his shivering horses shelter one cold, winter's night when he knocked at his door at the Bridge of Winter. There follows an analysis of the good and the evil in life. "The conscience of the wicked man destroys for himself the reality of Truth". At death, such a man's soul will "torment him with retributive vengeance at the Bridge of Judgement," (Ys.51.13).

Zarathushtra now praises some of his prominent followers. They are: Kavi Vishtaspa, his patron; the two brothers, Frashaoshtra and Jamaspa and lastly his own cousin, Maidhyomaongha the Spitama (Ys.51.16–19).

The concluding verses reaffirm Zarathushtra's faith in Ahura Mazda and His Powers (Ys.51.20–22).

Striving Towards the Spiritual Goal: Text
Yasna 51

1 He who serves with zeal
will receive the desired reward,
the bounty of Ahura Mazda's Sovereignty.
Man attains Truth by performing noble deeds.
From this very moment
I will establish the above as a certainty among us.

2 Truth is indeed primal for Ahura Mazda.
May Devotion reveal to me that longed-for Sovereignty
which is Yours.
May my prayers achieve the blessings of Your
Salvation through the Good Mind.

3 May those allied to You through their actions
listen to You,
O Ahura. Your very tongue is linked with Truth and
the Good Mind. You are the foremost Teacher
of these sublime doctrines.

4 Where does comfort replace sorrow?
Where does mercy prevail?
Where can Truth be attained?
Where is Your compassionate Devotion?
Where is Your Sovereignty,
O Mazda.
And where Your Supreme Mind?

5 All these I ask for.
Just as the good deeds
of the pious and intelligent herdsman dedicated to
Truth enables him to obtain his daily subsistence,
the cow,
so may law-abiding individuals
and their enlightened Guide, the Ratu,

through their penetrating insight,
control the two rewards (for good and evil).

6   The Sovereignty of Ahura Mazda
will be his who lavishes upon others
what is greater than the good as He wills.
But worse than evil
at the last turning point of existence[1] to him
who does not so dedicate his faith.

7   O Mazda,
You who have created the herds, the Waters and the
Plants,
grant me Perfection and Immortality
through Your Most Bountiful Spirit.
May I achieve moral courage and perseverance
through the teachings of the Good Mind.

8   Then indeed will I preach the doctrine for You,
O Mazda,
when man shall proclaim to the initiate
that evil comes to the evil but bliss to him who supports
Truth.
He who declares this Sacred Word
to the initiate undoubtedly rejoices Your Prophet,
the knowledgeable one.

9   Such just recompense You will give to both contenders,
O Mazda,
through Your blazing Fire and the ordeal of molten metal[2]
to be held up as a sign to the living.
Destruction upon the Followers of the Lie.
Salvation to the Followers of Truth.

10   But whoever seeks to destroy me,
apart from this Follower of the Lie,
is himself the offspring of an evil creation,
O Mazda.
Such men are ill-intentioned towards the living.

As for myself,
I invoke Truth that it may come to me
with the good reward.

11 What man is the ally of Spitama Zarathushtra,
O Mazda?
Who has taken counsel with Truth?
Who with loving Devotion?
What upright man
strives after the sacramental gift of the Good Mind?

12 (Not with such gifts) did the sodomite kavi
welcome Zarathushtra Spitama and his two shivering
horses
when they reached the Bridge of Winter[3]
(at dead of night) and were refused
hospitality and shelter.

13 The conscience of the wicked man
destroys for himself the reality of Truth.
His soul shall torment him with retributive vengeance
at the Bridge of the Separator, the Bridge of Judgement,
for his own deeds and his tongue strayed
from the path of Truth.

14 The Karapans are not submissive
to the principles of good husbandry.
They have condemned themselves
to be placed in the House of the Lie in the end
because of their injury to the herd
by their actions and beliefs.

15 Zarathushtra has promised the House of Song
as a reward to those sharing
the sacramental gift exchange.
(A magnificent gift), for Ahura Mazda was the first
to enter the House of Song.
O man,
this has been pledged to you for your salvation

because of your own Good Mind and Truth.

16   Through the power of the sacrament,
     and by following the path of the Good Mind,
     Kavi Vishtaspa has attained enlightenment
     by holding fast to the Truth.
     May Ahura Mazda,
     whose largesse knows no bounds,
     fulfil our ardent desire for bliss.

17   Frashaoshtra Hvogva has revealed to me his inner self
     as a token of his good conscience.
     May Mazda Ahura,
     through His Will,
     help him to follow in the footsteps of Truth.

18   Jamaspa Hvogva has coveted that enlightenment for his
     glory. His choice of Truth
     empowers him with the Good Mind.
     Grant me, O Ahura, that support which is Yours,
     O Mazda.

19   The heroic Maidhyomaongha Spitama[4]
     has joined me as well.
     The conscience of the initiate
     strives to attain the highest life.
     He will proclaim the Laws of Mazda
     having bettered material existence through his deeds.

20   O Sublime Powers,[5]
     all You who are of one accord, grant us this salvation.
     The words of Truth and the Good Mind
     are inspired by Devotion.
     With reverence we pray for their sustaining help,
     O Mazda.

21   Devotion makes man large hearted.
     Through his insight, words and actions his conscience
     will grow in Truth. Grant us,

O Mazda Ahura,
the Sovereignty of the Good Mind.
 I entreat You for this great boon.

22 Whoever is devoted to me and follows Truth
is looked upon as the best in worship.
Mazda Ahura knows those who have been and those
who are.
I invoke Him by His very own names
and embrace His Supreme Powers with love.[6]

Notes

1 See Ys.43.5, n.2 and Humbach, Gathas, p. 97, n. 5.

2 See Ys.32.7. n.3.

3 Bridge of Winter or Earth Bridge. Insler prefers the latter and asserts it is a place name. See Insler, *Gathas*, p. 105 and 316-317.

4 Maidhyomaongha or Maidhyoma was the first cousin and first disciple of Zarathushtra according to Pahlavi tradition. He is mentioned just this once in the Gathas.

5 Ahura Mazda and His Powers are addressed in the plural, but the verb is in the singular. See Yasmine Jhabvala, *Vers Ahura Mazda*, Bern, 1992, pp. 28, 150.

6 This is a puzzling verse. The last sentence, as rendered above, is an approximation. For variant readings, see Humbach, *Gathas, II,* p. 191. The *Yenghé hatam* prayer is based on this Gathic verse.

Gatha Vahishtoishti:

The Gatha of Fulfilment
The Marriage of Pouruchista
Yasna 53
Commentary

Between the Fourth and the Fifth Gatha, Ys.51 and 53, there is a gap. Yasna 52 is not in the Gathic Avestan dialect. It is a brief account of the various components of the human being: physical, mental, emotional and spiritual.

In spite of the oral tradition attributing it to the Prophet, the last Gatha, Ys.53, is a fragment of nine verses composed according to the style and content, after Zarathushtra's death, probably by a member of the Gatha Community.

This Gatha is often referred to as the Marriage Gatha, as it celebrates the marriage of Zarathushtra's youngest daughter, Pouruchista. It is also the Gatha of Fulfilment. (Ys.53.1–2).

The work of the Gatha Community is now revealed. Kavi Vishtaspa is addressed as "the spiritual heir of Zarathushtra" and invoked together with Frashaoshtra, close friend of the Prophet, to "establish the straight paths of the religion which Ahura has laid down for the Saviours."

The marriage ceremony begins. Pouruchista is requested to commune with her future husband whom Ahura has given to her "as a constant companion of the Good Mind, Truth and Wisdom." She is to perform benevolent acts by means of Armaiti, loving Devotion. She willingly agrees and prays to the Good Mind to dedicate her to the Beh-Deen, the excellent Religion, for all time (Ys.53.3–4).

The priest, or Pourichista herself, now addresses those present. Perhaps, this is a collective wedding, for "words of advice" are given to both brides and bridegrooms present. "May each of you strive with the other to attain Truth. Indeed, this will be to him, or her a blessed existence." Marriage, in Zoroastrianism, therefore, is looked upon as a sacramental bond (Ys.53.5).

The Followers of the Lie are warned they will lose all their earthly possessions, while Bliss (Ushta) will withdraw from those who scorn Righteousness. Their own actions will destroy the spiritual life for them (Ys.53.6).

Those who hold fast to their "sacramental vow", will chase away the Spirit of Deceit who, "dodging back and forth vanishes completely." Those who forsake their "sacramental trust" will cry "Woe" at the time of death (Ys.53.7).

"Corruption gnaws at those of evil choice. Such degenerates try to annihilate the right living." This refers to the wholesale massacre of innocent villagers, men, women and children, by marauding border tribes. The Gatha ends with the firm belief that Ahura Mazda will grant Sovereignty to the "upright Drighu" who are the oppressed and the forsaken crying out for justice (Ys.53.8–9).

The Marriage of Pouruchishta: Text
Yasna 53

1   The most ardent prayer of Spitama Zarathushtra has
    been heard.
    May Ahura Mazda,
    in harmony with Truth,
    grant him the blessing of the good life for all time.
    May this be given to those who,
    because of him, have understood and practised
    the words and deeds of the Good Religion.[1]

2   May Kavi Vishtaspa,
    the spiritual heir of Spitama Zarathushtra,
    and Frashaoshtra
    seek in thought, word and deed His fulness of Wisdom.
    May they have faith in the worship of Mazda
    and establish the straight paths of the Religion
    which Ahura has laid down for the Saviours.

3   O Pouruchista,[2]
    descendant of the Haechataspan Spitamas,
    and youngest of the daughters of Zarathushtra,
    Ahura has given you
    this man as a constant companion of the Good Mind,
    Truth,
    and Wisdom. So commune with him through your will,
    wisely performing the most benevolent acts of
    Devotion.

4   Indeed, I will love him
    be he father, husband, master of the herdsmen or
    member of the family. Being faithful to the righteous
    may the Sun-like heritage of Mazda's Good Mind
    dedicate me to the Good Religion for all time.

5   I[3] address words of advice to the brides and to you,
     O, bridegrooms,
     so listen carefully to these teachings.
     Being well versed in religious doctrines,
     learn to value the life of the Good Mind.
     May each of you strive with the other to attain Truth.
     Indeed, this will be to him or her
     a blessed existence.

6   In this way, O men and women,
     you will unite with Truth.
     Whatever you perceive to be advantageous to the
     seekers of the Lie,
     that shall be taken from them.
     Then they will be served with foul food and wail
     piteously. Bliss shall withdraw
     from those who scorn Righteousness.
     O evil ones, by your own actions you have destroyed
     the spiritual life for yourselves.

7   But the blessed recompense
     of holding fast to this sacramental vow
     will be yours, O brides and bridegrooms,
     so long as fervent love is rooted within you.
     Then the Spirit of Deceit, dodging back and forth,
     vanishes completely.
     Should you forsake this sacramental trust,
     then at the last gasp your cry will be "Woe!"

8   May all such workers of evil
     be crushed by their own deceits and perish howling.
     May good rulers inflict death upon them,
     but bring peace to the rejoicing villagers.
     Let the evil ones be confounded and laid low
     in the bonds of death, and let it be soon.

9   Corruption gnaws at those of evil choice.
     Such degenerates
     try to annihilate the right living.

Where is the Lord of Justice
who will deprive them of life and volition?
That, O Mazda, is Your Sovereignty
by which You grant the greater Glory
to the upright Drighu (the oppressed and the forsaken
crying out for justice).

Notes

1   Scholars are agreed that this Gatha is probably composed by a member of the Gatha community after Zarathushtra's death. The marriage of the Prophet's youngest daughter is being celebrated.

2   According to Pahlavi tradition, Zarathushtra had three sons and three daughters. The latter were: Freni, Thrithi and Pouruchista.

Jamaspa, a senior courtier at the court of Vishtaspa, is said to have married Pouruchista. Haechataspa was the fourth and Spitama the ninth ancestor of Zarathushtra according to Pahlavi Tradition.

3   It is not clear who is speaking, Pouruchista or the priest performing the ceremony.

Airyema Ishio Prayer

(Yasna 54.1 and 2)

Commentary

Yasna 54, named the *Airyema ishio* prayer after its opening lines, is traditionally held to be a powerful prayer for healing any sickness, physical or mental. There are just two paragraphs to this Yasna, and both form a fitting conclusion to the Gathas.

Again, as in *Yasna* 53, it is a member of the Gatha community who has probably composed the first paragraph. The Gatha community welcomes all friends of the new faith to join together to support the Good Mind. The conscience, or Daena, in every man helps him to earn the blessings which Ahura Mazda longs to bestow upon all mankind through Truth (Ys.54.1).

In the second paragraph, composed centuries later, the devotees burst into ecstatic adoration of the Gathas and of the thirty-three different texts of the *Staota Yasna*, which include the Gathas.

The Gathas are exalted not only for being pure and holy, but for their inherent power of ruling as enlightened Guides leading mankind to their destined goal, the Frashokéréti, "the wondrous renewal of existence" (Ys.54.2).

Hence the importance of the Gathas in the Zoroastrian tradition. They are not only the most ancient among the Sacred Texts, but also the most important because of the teachings they embody. They have survived from prehistoric times through their constant recitation, by priest and laity, especially during the days in remembrance of the righteous dead. To this day the Gathas are recited annually for five consecutive days not only in every fire temple, but also in some private homes. A room is set apart for the priest and the family to welcome the Fravashis of all loved ones. The room is washed, a clean sheet placed on the ground, an

Afarghan or fire censer piled with sandalwood and incense is lighted and kept burning. Marble-topped tables are laid with gleaming silver vases filled with fresh flowers each vase consecrated to the memory of the beloved dead. The bare wall of the room facing the priest is festooned with garlands of fresh flowers, scented white tube roses or yellow jasmine intertwined with pink and red roses. The flickering fire light from the afarghan, the scent of incense and flowers mingling with the chanting of the prayers are memories clinging to every traditional Parsi home at the time of the Farvardegan days.

Airyema Ishio Prayer
Yasna 54.1 and 2

May the purposeful assembly of the Arya clan,
gathered here to support the men and women of
Zarathushtra uphold the chosen religion of the Good Mind
which brings its own rich award.
I will entreat Truth for that great blessing
which Ahura Mazda longs to bestow (upon us all) (Ys.54.1).

We revere the Airyema Ishio prayer,
the powerful, victorious against the evil minded,
the greatest of the chants dedicated to Truth.
We adore the pure and holy Gathas
ruling as enlightened guides for mankind.
We praise the Staota Yasna[1] hymns which embody
the Primal Laws of Life (Ys.54.2).

Notes

1 The Staota Yasna hymns consist
   of thirty–three different texts,
   including the Gathas.

Transliteration of the Text
Yasna 54

1   a airyema ishio rafedhrai jantu
nérébyascha nairibyascha Zarathushtrahé
vanghéush rafedhrao mananghao ya Daena
vairim hanat mizhdem. Ashaya yasa Ashim
yam ishyam Ahuro masata Mazdao

2   Airyamanem ishim yazamaidé, amavantem,
véréthrajanem, vitbaéshanghem,
mazishtem Ashahé sravangham.
Gathao spentao ratu-kshathrao ashaonish yazamaidé.
Staota yesnya yazamaide ya data anghaush paouruyehya.

Glossary

Afarghan: Large metallic fire-censer in which the consecrated Fire of Zoroastrian Temples is placed. Smaller Afarghans used for fires lit in houses on special occasions such as birthdays, wedding anniversaries and the ten day Farvardegan Ceremonies in remembrance of the virtuous dead.

Ahu: Eternal Life, an epithet of Ahura Mazda, Lord of Life and Wisdom.

Ahum Bis: Healer of Life, title reserved for Ahura Mazda and Zarathushtra. Associated with Ratu, the enlightened Guide (Vedic *Guru*).

Ahura: Lord of Life, the Zoroastrian name for God. See Mazda.

Ahura Mazda: Lord of Life and Wisdom,

Airyama: Aryan clan see Khvétu, and Verézéna

Airyana Vaeja: The Land of the Aryans, Iran.

Ajyaiti: Non-life, linked with Gaya, mortal life

Ako Mana: Evil Mind, opposite of Vohu Mana, Good Mind.

Ameretat/Amardad: Immortality. Twin of Haurvatat, Perfection. One of the Amesha Spenta. Vedic *Amrutatat*, Immortality. *Amrut*, nectar.

Amesha Spenta/Amshaspands: Immortal Shining Ones emanating from Ahura Mazda through whom He rules Man, Nature and the Cosmos.

Anagra Raochao: Everlasting light where Ahura Mazda dwells.

Angra Mainyu: Hostile Spirit. Also called Ahriman. Opposite of SPENTA MAINYU, Benevolent Spirit, Holy Spirit.

Armaiti: Devotion, Love, Piety, Zeal. One of the Amesha Spenta. Vedic *Aramati*.

Asha: Cosmic Order, Truth, Justice, Righteousness. One of the Amesha Spenta. Vedic *Rta*.

Asha Vahishta: Highest Asha, emblem of the consecrated Fire.

Ashavan: Follower of Truth, Seeker after Truth.

Ashi Vanghui (fem.): Ashi the Good, represents material and spiritual wealth to be offered by every Zoroastrian to Ahura Mazda.

Aspa Siha: Black Horse, favourite stallion of Kavi Vishtaspa.

Astavant/Azdebish: Bones, flesh, blood, etc. See BODY.

Asuras: Vedic name for the high gods of Truth and Justice, later demonised in Hindu texts.

Asvins (Skt.): Twin Horsemen in the Vedas who bring to mankind *madhu vidya*, the honey-sweet knowledge of Divinity.

Atar/Atash/Adar: Fire. Held sacred as an emblem of Ahura Mazda. Installed with elaborate rituals, in Zoroastrian Fire Temples.

Atash Adaran: Fire of Fires. Second Grade of Zoroastrian Fire Temple.

Atash Behram: Fire of Victory. First grade of Zoroastrian Fire Temple.

Atash Dadgah/Agiary: Third grade of Zoroastrian Fire Temple. Also describes the household Fire.

Atash Khoreh: Glorious Fire. Exalted title given to the Sacred Fire. Linked with Hvaré Shaetha, Resplendent Sun.

Avesta: Collective name for the Zoroastrian Scriptures. Also name of the language in which Avestan Texts are written.

Bang/Bhang: Narcotic plant.

Baodha: Discerning Intellect. Cf. Vedic *Buddhi*.

Barsam/Barsom: Sacred plant whose twigs were used in Zoroastrian rituals in ancient Iran. Today replaced by thin, metallic wires.

Body (Human): Made up of 9 parts described in Ys.55.1.

I.		Purely Material and Perishable:
	(a)	GAETHA, primal, physical elements;
	(b)	ASTAVANT/AZDEBISH, bones blood, tissues
	(c)	TANVAS, entire physique. Personality.
II.		Mixture of the gross and the subtle:

(a) USHTANA, the life breath which at death returns to the atmosphere whence it came;

(b) KEHRPA, the luminous body beneath the physical body. At death, returns to the Sun whence it came.

(c) TEVISHI, Desire, longing which can reach up to Perfection, or descend into brutality.

III. Eternal elements not destroyed at time of physical death:

(a) BAODHA (Vedic *Buddhi*), the discerning intellect;

(b) URVAN/RUAN, the Soul;

(c) FRAVASHI/FAROHAR, the eternal, incorruptible spark of Ahura Mazda which guides and protects humans, animals, plants and the cosmos.

Boi Ceremony: Ritual feeding of the Sacred Fire in the Fire Temples, three to five times a day, with sandalwood and incense, by the Priest in charge.

Chinvat Bridge: Bridge of Judgment, to be crossed by all souls at death. Also described as CHINVATO PERETU, the Bridge of the Separation, separating good from evil.

Chisti/Chista (fem.): Luminous insight, HU-CHISTI, the Good Chisti linked with HU-KHRATU, the good Intellect, and OYA-CHISTI, unique insight.

Dacna/Deen: Visionary perception or conscience in man. Later named Beh Deen, the Good Religion.

Daevas: Shining ones in the Vedas, but stigmatised by Zarathushtra as False Gods, and Worshippers of False Gods.

Dakhyu: The country, the fourth regional group into which Iran was divided.

Demana/Nmana: House or home, the first of the four regional groups into which the country was divided.

Divo/Diva: A small lighted wick floating in a glass of oil. Essential during Zoroastrian ceremonies, and also at home when the individual prays for an hour or more. Fire is the essential witness to the prayers recited. Cf. Vedic *Agni shakshi*,

Dregvant: Follower of the DRUJ or Lie.

Drighu: The poor and the oppressed to whom injustice has been done. Zarathushtra identifies himself with the Drighu.

Dron/Darun: Unleavend bread consecrated and eaten at the Yasna Ceremony.

Druj: The Lie.

Drujo Demana: House of the Lie, i.e. Hell.

Duraosha: "Keeping Death afar," an epithet of the sacred plant, Haoma, Vedic *Soma*, used in both Vedic and Zoroastrian rituals to this day.

Ereshi: Vedic Rishi.

Farishta: An angelic being, a messenger of the Divine.

Fashuyente: Herdsman linked with Vastrya, shepherd or husbandman.

Frashokéréti: The Renewal of Man, Nature and the Cosmos at the end of Time.

Fravashi/Farohar: The Protective Guardian Spirit in man, nature, animals, and the entire cosmos.

Gaetha: The primal elements of the human body.

Gah/Gehs: The five divisions into which the 24 hours are divided for prayer.

Garo Demana: House of Song, Heaven, signifying Bliss.

Gaush Tasha: He who moulds or shapes the Cow/Ox/Bull/Cattle.

Gaush Urva: Lit. Soul of the Cow/Ox/Bull/Cattle

(1) Symbol for Mother Earth

(2) Associated with light. "Cows of dawn". "bulls of the days", (Vedic Images)

(3) Honoured as an Amesha Spenta

(4) Protector of all Four-footed animals.

(5) Her powerful voice represents the cry of the oppressed demanding justice.

(6) Represents life itself. (Ys, 33.4, 44.6,47.3)

Gava Azi: Cow-in-calf, symbol of prosperity and plenty.

Gaya: Mortal, physical life which disappears at death.

Gayodad: Primeval Bull.

Gayomard: Primeval Man.

Getig: Physical world of matter. Opposite of MENOG, the mental world.

Grehma: Loot or ill-gotten gains.

Guzra Sengha: Profound teachings. Popularly held to be secret doctrines.

Ha/Haiti: Chapter or chapters into which the *Yasna* is divided.

Hakim: Physician, herbalist.

Hamazor: Spiritual handclasp.

Hamkar: Fellow-worker with Ahura Mazda.

Haoma: Vedic *soma*, the sacred plant whose juice is used in Zoroastrian and Vedic rituals even to this day.

Haurvatat: Vedic *Sarvatat*, Perfection, an Amesha Spenta

Huiti: Craftsman

Hvare Kshaeta: The Resplendent Sun, linked with Atash Khoreh, Glorious Fire.

Iblis: Muslim name for Satan.

Ijashne: See YASNA.

Indra: Patron god of young men, specially warriors.

Jama-Pichori: Priestly robes of a Zoroastrian priest.

Karapans/Karap: Lit. "mumbler priests," who assisted the Zaotar or Chief Priest at the ritual and the sacrifice.

Kavis: The princelings of Zarathushtra's day.

Khashathra: Sovereignty, Power, Kingdom, an Amesha Spenta.

Khratu: Intellect in man also the will or purpose of Ahura Mazda. *Hukhratu*, the Good Intellect, is linked with Mazda's Wisdom, and with Vohu Mana, Good Mind. *Dush-Khratu*, the Evil Intellect

misleads man making him plan evil and destruction.

Khoreh/Khvarnah: Kingly glory.

Khvetu: The self-reliant, the first of the four grades of Zarathushtra's followers.

Kushti/Kusti: The sacred thread worn round the waist over the sacred shirt, Sudra/Sudreh, by every devout Zoroastrian.

Lucifer: Judaic name for Satan.

Maga: Sacramental gift exchange.

Magavan: A practitioner of the sacramental gift exchange. MAGI later form of MAGAVAN.

Mainyu (Twin): Twin Spirits or Mentalities. *Spenta Mainyu*, Spirit of Benediction, *Spenishta Mainyu*, Most Holy Spirit, epithet of Ahura Mazda alone. *Angra Mainyu*, Hostile or Evil Spirit, the Spirit of destruction who will be annihilated at the end of Time.

Mairya/Marya: Young men, warriors, whose patron god was Indra.

Mana/Manangha/Manas: The mind in human beings. Associated with VOHU MANA, Good Mind, VAHISHTA MANA Supreme Mind, attribute of AHURA MAZDA alone; SUCHA MANANGHA, illumined mind; ACHISTA MANA, darkened mind, attribute of ANGRA MAINYU, the Evil Spirit.

Manthra: The Sacred Word of Power embodied in the Scriptures. Vedic *mantra*.

Manthran: Preacher of the Sacred Word of Power.

Mara: Buddhist name for Satan.

Mazda: Wisdom, linked with AHURA. Vedic Médha.

Motto of the Religion: Humata , Good Thoughts; Hukhta, Good Words; Huvarashta, Good Deeds.

Nasks: Religious compilations of the Sasanian Era (224-651AC), 21 in number: seven on Religion; seven on Law and Order; seven on Medicine. Originals are lost but lengthy summaries exist in various Pahlavi Texts.

Ordeal: By Fire and molten metal.

Pahlavi: Written language of the Sasanians.

Pairimaiti: Devious thinking, opposite of ARMAITI.

Pazand: Spoken language of the Sasanians.

Raam/Mino Raam: Spirit of abounding peace.

Rata: Spirit of religious generosity.

Ratheshtar: Warrior.

Ratu: Vedic *Guru*, the enlightened Guide to Salvation.

Saoshyant: Saviour, all good men regarded as active saviours.

Saoshyos: Future saviour to be born at the end of time.

Sasna: Sacred doctrines

Sava: Salvation.

Sengha: Sacred teachings.

Shoithra/Zantu: Province or state.

Shyothena: Action, linked with MANA, thought, and VACHA, word.

Spenta: Benevolent, sacred.

Sraosha: Inward hearing, hearkening to Ahura Mazda. Obedience to Will of Ahura Mazda, Inspiration, Discipline.

Taromaiti: Cussedness, obstinacy. Opposite of ARMAITI, right thinking,

Tevishi: Vedic *Tavishi*. Root meaning, brutality. Also represents intense desire for good or evil.

Tushnamaiti: Explained by Pahlavi writers as "silent, meditative thought leading to Armaiti, perfect thought."

Ughda: Inspired word of religious poetry.

Ukshano Asnam: Lit. Bulls of the Days. (Vedic image) Refers to a new dawn to be ushered in by the Saoshyants.

Urva: Soul in humans and animals.

Ushta: Bliss.

Usig/Usiksh: Name of tribe who introduced the worship of *Agni*, Fire, among the Vedic Indians.

Utauiti: Strength, endurance, power. Linked withTevishi.

Vacha: The spoken word of everyday speech.

Vérézéna: Community. Second grade of Zarathushtra's followers.

Vidhvao: The learned individual, the initiate.

Vis: Town. Second of the four regional groups in Zarathushtra's day.

Vohu Mana: Good Mind. One of the Amesha Spenta.

Yasna: Lit. worship. Ritual text of 72 Haiti or chapters, including the Gathas.

Yazada/Yazata: Angelic being. Personification of the elements Fire, Water, Earth, Wind, Sky, Stars, etc., and abstract qualities in Man, e.g. Sraosha, Raam.

Zand/Zend: Commentary on the Avesta.

Zaotar: Officiating priest at a ritual.

Brief Bibliography

Prehistory

Archaeologische Mitteilungen aus Iran, New Series, Berlin, 1968ff.

Bahn (Paul G.) *The Cambridge Illustrated History of Archaeology,* Cambridge, 1996.
The Cambridge Illustrated History of Prehistoric Art, Cambridge, 1998.

Childe (V. Gordon), *New Light on the Most Ancient East,* rewritten 1952 Routledge, London.

Ghirshman (Roman), *Iran* from the earliest time till the Islamic Conquest, Penguin, 1954, paperback.

Herzfeld (Ernst), *Archaeological History of Iran,* Oxford University Press, Oxford, 1935; *Iran in the Ancient East,* OUP, Oxford, 1941.

Historical Background

Frye (Richard N.) *The History of Ancient Iran,* C.H.Beck, Munich, 1984.

Gnoli (Gherardo N.), "Zoroaster's Time and Homeland", *Seminario di Studi Asiatici,* No.7, Instituto Universitario Orientale, Naples, 1980.

Yarshater (Ehsan), General Editor, *The New Cambridge History of Ancient Iran.*

Biography

Jackson (A.V. Williams), *Zoroaster, the Prophet of Ancient Iran,* Macmillan, New York, 1899, London, 1901, Reprint, AMS Press, 1965.

Molé (Marijan), *La Legende de Zoroastre,* Klincksieck, Paris, 1967.

Religious Background

Anklesaria (Behramgore Tehmuras), *Zand–Akasih*, Iranian or Greater Bundahishn, (Book of Creation), Transliteration and Translation in English, Rahnumae Mazdayasnan Sabha, Bombay, 1956.

Boyce (Mary), *A History of Zoroastrianism,* B.J. Brill, Leiden, Vol.I, 1975, Reprint 1989.
Zoroastrianism, its Antiquity and Constant Vigour, Columbia Lectures on Iranian Studies, No.7, Mazda Publishers, Costa Rica, California, U.S.A. 1992.

Bulsara (Sohrab Jamshedjee), Tr. *Aerpatastan and Nirangistan*, Bombay, 1921.

Dhalla (M.N.),*Zoroastrian Theology, from the earliest times to the present day*, New York, 1914.

Duchesne Guillemin (Jacques), *The Religion of Ancient Iran*, tr.from the French by Dastur K. M. Jamaspasa, Tata Press, Bombay, 1973.

Eliade (Mircea), *A History of Religious Ideas*, Collins, London, 1979 Vol.I.

Hume (R.E.) *The Thirteen Principal Upanishads*, Oxford, 1921.

Jhabvala (Yasmine), *Vers Ahura Mazda*, Peter Lang, Bern, 1992.

Lommel (Herman), *Die Religion Zarathushtras nach dem Awesta,* Mohr, Tubingen, 1930; Reprint, Georg Olms, 1971.

Modi (J.J.), *The Religious Ceremonies and Customs of the Parsees*, Bombay, Reprint, 1986.

Mokhri (Mohammad), *La Lumiere et le Feu dans l'Iran ancien*,Leuven, 2nd.ed. 1982.

Mole (Marijan), *Culte, Mythe et Cosmogonie dans l'ran ancien*, Presses Universitaires de France, Paris 1963.

Moulton (James), *Early Zoroastrianism*, London, Williams and Norgate, 1913 rpt AMS, 1972

Nyberg (H.S.), *Die Religionen des alten Iran,* J. C. Hinrichs, Leipzig, 1938; Reprint, Zeller, 1966.

Tagore (Rabindranath), *The Religion of Man,* Hibbert Lectures, 1930. First pub. 1931. This ed. Allen and Unwin London, 1967. Paperback.

Vahman (Fereydun), *Arda Wiraz Namag*, Text and translation, Curzon Press, London, 1986.

Varenne (Jean), *Zarathushtra et la tradition mazdeenne*, Edition Seuil, Paris, 1966.

Critical Translations

Darmesteter (J), *Le Zend Avesta*, 3 vols. Tr.L.H. Mills SBE Vols. 4, 23, 31, Motilal Banarasidass, Delhi, 1965.

Duchesne Guillemin (Jacques), *The Hymns of Zarathushtra,* tr. from the French by Mrs. M. Henning, Wisdom of the East Series, John Murray, London 1952. Reprint, 1992.

Humbach (Helmut), *Die Gathas des Zarathushtra,*

2 Vols. C. Winter, Heidelberg, 1959. Humbach, Elfenbein and Skjaerve, *The Gathas of Zarathushtra,* 2 Vols. 1991. Humbach and Pallan Ichaporia, *The Heritage of Zarathushtra* C. Winter, Heidelberg, 1994, paperback.

Insler (Stanley), *The Gathas of Zarathushtra,* Acta Iranica, No.8, E.J. Brill, Leiden, 1975.

Kellens (Jean) and Pirart (Eric), *Les Textes Vieil-Avestique,* Vol. I, Dr. Ludwig Reichart Verlag, Wiesbaden, 1988. Vol.II, TVA, 1990.

Lommel (Herman), *Die Gathas des Zarathushtra,* Schwabe, Basel, 1971 (excluding *Yasna* 53, the last Gatha).

Monna (Maria C.), *The Gathas of Zarathushtra:* a Reconstruction of the Text, Rodopi, Amsterdam, 1978.

Smith (Maria Wilkins), *Studies in the Syntax of the Gathas of Zarathushtra,* Philadelphia, 1929; Reprint, New York, 1966.

Taraporewala (Irach J.S.), *The Divine Songs of Zarathushtra, a Philological Study,* D.B. Taraporewala and Sons, Bombay, 1951. Reprint, Hukhta Foundation, Bombay, 1996.

Contemporary Paperback Volumes, informative and enjoyable:

Irani (D.J.), *Understanding the Gathas: the Hymns of Zarathushtra,* Ahura Publishers, Womelsdorf, 1994.

Mehr (Farhang), *The Zoroastrian Tradition, an Introduction to the Ancient Wisdom of Zarathushtra,* Element Inc. U.S.A. 1991, and Element Books, Great Britain, 1991.

Nigosian (S.A.), *The Zoroastrian Faith, Tradition and Modern Research,* McGill Queen's University Press, Montreal and London, 1993.

Centres of Excellence for Zoroastrian Research

The Asiatic Society of Bombay, Bombay, India.

K. R. Cama Oriental Institute, Bombay, India.\

Meherji Rana Collection of Manuscripts, Meherji Rana Library, Navsari. India.

Royal Asiatic Society Library, London, U.K.

School of Oriental and African Studies, University of London, U.K.

Department of Comparative Religion, University of Manchester, U.K.

Department of Comparative Religion, Columbia University, New York, U.S.A.

Department of Comparative Religion, Ontario University, Canada.

An Annotated Bibliography on Zoroastrian Studies, compiled by Asha Gupta, Indira Gandhi National Centre for the Arts, New Delhi, 1998. A unique compilation giving cross references to material on Zoroastrian themes found in libraries and institutions in and around Delhi.

Index